THERE GOES THE NEIGHBORHOOD!

Mark Stephen Clifton

Copyright 1993, Mark Stephen Clifton

Updated Edition 2018

Published by HICKEY & McGEE

hickeybooks.com

An enterprise of

PERELANDRA COLLEGE

8697-C La Mesa Boulevard, PMB 21

La Mesa, California 91942

perelandra.edu

ISBN: 10: 1983426261

ISBN 13: 9781983426261

BISAC: TRU000000 - TRUE CRIME / General

Cover Art by Rod Legace

For Buddy Blue, Celeste Teresa Cecil Montalvo-Jackson, and the San Carlos Survivors

TABLE OF CONTENTS

INTRODUCTION

"Little white houses in neat little rows, contrasting against the sky." The Animals

I remember a long, thirsty hike I made up Cowles Mountain when I was not quite five years old. At that time it seemed that my dad, my sister, and I were on a journey to the top of the world. Each plateau should have been the top, but it wasn't. I think Dad underestimated the toughness and steepness of the terrain. At that time, there were no trails.

The age-old question of every youth must have come from me that day: "Are we there yet?" Not having a canteen complicated matters, but finally we reached the top! I was sure God lived up there. To the west was the Pacific Ocean, to the east, the Laguna Mountains.

What really captivated me was directly below: rows and rows of houses that looked exactly the same. I saw the big, flat area of my soon-to-be school, Cleveland Elementary. It was such a serene picture that none of us caught a glimpse of the black, consuming cloud that was to over-shadow the community.

The year was 1960.

CHAPTER 1

THE END OF INNOCENCE

"I smoked my first cigarette at ten, and for girls I had a bad yen. When I was young." The Animals

Lake Arianna Drive was a neatly arranged street with brand-new lawns and trees signifying someone else had just purchased a new home. I was five-years-old and beginning to make friends with other kids. It seemed like every house on the street had a couple of sons and daughters about the same age. It was a ready-made gang.

Since it was late August, I was getting excited about going to kindergarten. My parents kept hyping it up so, naturally, I was filled with anticipation. My sister had just finished first grade, so I had an inside connection on what school would really be like.

A couple of houses up the street lived a kid who always had the newest anything that came out — clothes, tricycles, whatever. One unmistakable characteristic was his addiction to candy. Greg always had some form of sucrose hanging out of his mouth. I wondered why he was so hyper. If you looked in the dictionary under "towhead," Greg Hayes would be pictured. His hair was as white as snow.

Greg's parents were always nice to me. His dad was a

gruff kind of a guy, plumber by trade, and his mom was a very pretty and petite blonde. (I had known what a good-looking female was ever since I could walk.) Greg was slightly younger than me, yet we had become friends. Greg, like every kid, tested the boundaries of friendship. I think he had a latent desire to rule and manipulate, divide and conquer, at a very young age. One day Greg took my tricycle. I wasn't too upset about it, but my mom, defender of the universe, told me to get it back: "Don't let anyone push you around. Go slug that kid if you need to, but get your trike back!" she commanded. These words seem to become a lifetime battle cry. (Not the "get your trike back" part of course.] They were more than words. They were my confidence, my justification, and my empowerment, which was ironic, since in future years, most of what came out of my mother's mouth was negative and destructive.

I found Greg that day and I warned him with my new found boldness, "Give me my trike back, or I'll beat you up!" Greg didn't budge, so I gave him a right fist to the head. My only experience with fighting up to this point had been watching Popeye smash the bad guys. I gave Greg my best Popeye-to-Bluto imitation. Greg didn't say a word, but ran home crying. The next day we were friends again, but our roles were swapped. I didn't lord it over him for long though. I didn't know it, but in a few short days, I would be on the receiving of another five-year-old's fist.

Greg and I were friends throughout elementary school.

He was younger, and I had other friends my age, and we hung out often. We built forts, discovered the freedom of peeing on bushes, and like all the luckiest kids in Southern California, got to live mostly outdoors.

In 1960, San Carlos was a series of tract homes in the boonies. There were plenty of hills, trails, and wilderness places in which a young boy could run wild. Greg's dad built dune buggies for a hobby and he also kept a boat docked at the Colorado River. The river was in the middle of the desert of California and Arizona. If you were one of the "chosen," you would get invited to go to the sand dunes and the river with the Hayes family. I went a couple of times. Hitting the dunes and trails in one of the dune buggies was the ultimate thrill. Greg shared his dad's love of the adrenaline rush!

Mr. Hayes made Greg a copy of a "Sting Ray" bike with the banana seat and a sissy bar. All the kids drooled over it. He would let me ride it at times. Behind Grover Cleveland Elementary were some huge hills where houses were going to be built, but for some reason, the money for the project dried up. The bulldozers had done their part, but no construction had begun. So the hills were excellent for speed and jumps on a bike. One Saturday afternoon we thought we would ride double down the steepest and bumpiest hill. I felt the wind in my face blurring my vision as I rode up on the handlebars with Greg on the seat. In the twinkling of an eye, we were airborne!

4

SMASH!

I landed on my face, and for some reason, didn't move. Shock, probably.

Greg got up and was walking and sobbing at the same time. A neighbor, who had seen the whole thing, gave Greg and me a ride home in his truck, with our mangled bike in back.

I went to the doctor and he said that I was lucky I had braces on my on my teeth, or they would have been knocked out. It's a wonder any of us survived the era of no bike helmets or pads! Greg, forever the dare devil, and I, were back at the same trails the next week. Our parents didn't know.

Greg would later perish in a motorcycle accident in L.A. and leave behind a son. There's probably some toe-headed teen with the last name of Hayes somewhere in Southern California doing outrageous things on a skateboard or motor cross.

Life in elementary school was fun for the most part, but there were some extremely sad times with my mother's bi-polar condition (called manic-depression back then) coming to the surface. The only breath of fresh air was hanging out with my friends, studying in my room, or taking summer vacations with my dad and my sister. We generally went without my mom, at her request.

I remember one time playing with Play-Doh on the driveway when my mother went into a rampage for some unknown reason. She was screaming, cursing, and yelling things at me that no child should hear. My dad pulled up and seemed to grasp what was going on, because I sure didn't. He said, "Let the kids alone, they're only young once. Let them be kids!" I have never forgotten that.

The innocence of childhood was quickly evaporating like morning dew on the grass.

Pershing Junior High seemed like a place of constant excitement, joy, fear, identity crisis, and an endless supply of cute girls who held my heart in their hands. After finally establishing a firm base of security at Cleveland Elementary with friends I had grown close to from kindergarten on, all of a sudden I was thrust into this whirlwind of 3000 or more hormone-filled peers, and starting over. After being a big shot sixth grader at Cleveland Elementary, I was low man on the totem pole.

The ninth graders seemed like giants, too cool and too tough to associate with us "pea-greeners". One such person was Duke Miller, the embodiment of all you hated and all you wanted to be. He was part of the Cowles Mountain gang that I was just getting to know. Our first meeting went something like this: "Hey, punk, I'll fight you on my knees!" My new friend Stan just happened to be walking with me. He knew Duke well, and convinced him I was "cool."

Stan was another interesting person, a seventh grader with a vision. I entered into a plan to run away to Haight-

Ashbury with him that summer of 1968. It seemed like that's all we talked and dreamed about! "Mark, on the way to San Francisco, let's stop in Los Angeles and see the Playboy Playmate of the year. She lives up there some place," Stan said. Reality didn't seem to affect us much.

I was excited but a bit apprehensive. "Do you think she would want to see us?" I asked.

"You bet. 'Free Love' is in."

Stan was always confident. I wasn't quite sure about this, but the man had a plan!

We were very interested in not living at our respective homes with our parents. My father was the solid rock in our family, but we seemed to be losing touch. My mother's manic-depression kept getting worse. I later learned from my grandmother that when Mom was a child, they didn't know how to deal with this disorder, so doctors told her parents not to discipline her, or she might "wig out." Well, she wigged out anyway.

She attempted suicide many times when I was growing up. I can remember times that I would just pound my fists against the wall at night and try to plug my ears to get away from her constant babbling and accusations. I had a little transistor radio I would use with ear phones to block out the insanity. Her Valiums, which the doctors prescribed upon her requests, mixed with her alcohol, did anything but calm her down.

My father often worked nights and didn't know all the

strange things that she did in his absence. Pop worked hard all his life, fought in two wars, had a second career in the custodial field for the city schools, and just wanted a happy family. I think my mother did also, but she couldn't control what was happening on the inside. We seemed to become enemies. I gave up on her, and she gave up on me. In the process of discarding her bad attributes, I discarded anything good she had to say. I saw her as a roadblock to growing up, a barrier to freedom and identity. The problem was, I threw away any rational counsel at the same time. I was going to make my own rules. The result was anarchy.

Stan hated his dad. I couldn't for the life of me figure out why. His family took me deep sea fishing and to Mission Bay for ski-surfing on the wakes of their boat; we didn't have any water skis, so we used an old ten-foot Hobie surfboard to surf the wakes after letting go of the rope. They seemed like a great family.

Stan had a lot of freedom, but inside he had this self-constructed wall that caused many problems. Stan could be a very malicious kid. He did senseless vandalism, in which, of course, I joined him. We chain-smoked cigarettes. I remember sticking our hands under cigarette machines and pulling packs of Marlboros or Camel non-filters down. Stan loved to steal things. He was an average student, but I could see much deeper than his report cards. Stan was a very bright kid who didn't care to apply himself at all.

I wasn't into stealing, but when I hung out with Stan, it was a way of life. We were walking through Mission Valley in between hitching rides to see a movie, and we found a boat with belongings in it. I stole the wallet that was there. I thought back then that it was a stupid and senseless act, but I thought being accepted was more important than any values.

Our trip to Haight-Ashbury never happened. I was ready to go, but Stan gave me some half-baked reason why he couldn't do it. We started growing apart, and Stan began hanging out with another guy our age, Bruce, who lived two doors down from me.

One sunny morning on the way to eighth grade, I stopped at the 7-11 convenience store to get my daily ration of candy. Bruce and Stan were together, and Stan said he wanted to fight me. I was taken back because I still considered us to be friends. Bruce gave Stanley two chains with heavy led weights soldered to them.

"Take your pick," Stan said to me as if I was choosing from two pieces of beef jerky.

I had a sense of honor that bordered on stupidity. I retorted, "I'll fight you with my fists."

We proceeded to the back of the convenience store, and by that time it seemed that at least 100 fellow students were watching: The "Animal", Jon Jackson, and David Lucas were among the onlookers. Stan swung his chain

around as if he were Batman with his bat hook. "Smash!"
It whacked my skull. With every hit to my head I
responded with a punch to his face. I remember some girl
yelling at Stan and calling him a wimp in so many words.
This exchange went on for some time until finally, we both
stopped. My head was badly bleeding, as was Stan's face. I
was extremely dizzy, but I proceeded to school.

My first class was algebra, and I didn't want to sit too
close to the front. The teacher's name was Mrs. Knee. She
adamantly opposed the up and coming drug culture. I can
remember one poster in her room: "FLOWER CHILDREN
WHO SMOKE POT END UP BECOMING BLOOMING
IDIOTS." Mrs. Knee was a concerned teacher who was
good-looking, married and drove fast cars. For some
unknown reason, she committed suicide not too long after
this. Anyway, she didn't question why my head was
smashed in. I actually had a not-so-minor concussion.

I remember trying to figure out the fight. I had taken
Stan bowling that previous summer, and we had ended up
wrestling in the alley. I had pinned him, but all in fun, I
thought. Maybe not in his mind. Anyway, it was a moral
victory for me. I was establishing myself as not only "one
of the guys," but as one of the "tough" guys. It was worth
the headache.

When I was around twenty years old, I saw Stan at a
keg party in Point Loma. He had just gotten married, he
was getting along with his dad, and he had quit drugs,

"except for a little coke once in a while". We all knew it was a "harmless" drug at this time.

A few months later Stan was stabbed to death behind a discotheque a stone's throw from the 7-11 where we had our duel. Rumor had it he was killed over a cocaine deal gone awry. So much for the harmless drug. When I heard this, an old saying rang through my mind: "He who lives by the sword will die by the sword."

The black cloud that nurtured its garden of violence, also demanded a harvest.

CHAPTER 2

A FOUNDATION OF VIOLENCE; THE MAKING OF "THE ANIMAL"

"Summer's here and the time is right for fighting in the streets, boys." The Rolling Stones

I vividly remember another incident that happened in eighth grade. I had made a friend the year before in one of my classes. His name was Steve and he was tall, in good shape, and supposed to be the toughest guy in our grade. My school, Pershing Jr. High, was no small school. There were at least 1000 students in eighth grade alone. Steve and I had gotten along well, and had a mutual acceptance of one another. Then the "too cool" monster consumed him.

In Mrs. Knee's algebra class Steve and I sat near each other. All of a sudden his friendship turned to animosity. Steve said I looked like a raisin. That hurt. I do possess dark features and a kind of hook nose.

I remembered back to the year before, when another one of my best friends was after the same girl I was, Alyssa. In order to impress her, he started putting down my nose while we three were walking home from school.

I remember lying awake at nights and using my hand

to try to push my nose into an upright position. It didn't work, needless to say, and I had to learn to live with this object — in the middle of my face — that looks like the plastic nose attached to the glasses and eyebrows in the Five and Dime stores.

It seemed I was always on the receiving end of peer sabotage. When I was in the sixth grade I had a girl friend who was a year younger. Her name was Linda Provost and she had met me when I was pushing her little brother around. She had told me to pick on someone my own size and by the next week I had given her my Maltese Cross and Saint Christopher medal. This was serious stuff.

One day I was going to kiss her for the first time. I took her out to the side of her house. Usually only her sisters were home. Her mom was a single mother of five kids, and she worked all the time. "Linda, I really like you a lot...," I said in a crackling kind of pre-adolescent way.

I grabbed her hands, and she said, "Go ahead and say it, Mark." Then I muttered, "Well..., oh never mind." Anyway, I chickened out. She was ready and willing but I lost my nerve. We went together for a few months, which is forever to a couple who are eleven and twelve years old. I had her over to my house to listen to my Four Seasons records and my new Monkees albums. I think she loved me.

One day at school, a girl named Laurie came up to me and said she wondered why I would go steady with someone so young. I agreed, and said I should break up with her. What an idiot I was. Laurie said, "Don't worry, I'll tell her." I remember seeing Linda. She was a sight to behold with her beautiful blue eyes full of tears and her face covered with her flowing blonde hair. I never talked to her again. I thought this would be a great opportunity to ask Laurie to go steady with me. She said "No way." Until this day I think she had a hidden agenda. There I was — womanless and feeling very stupid.

Nine years later I got the news that Linda had died of a heroin overdose in northern California. What part did I play in her final act of desperation? What part did her father, who had left her, play? I'll never know, but there is still a sinking feeling in my heart when I think about her.

Anyway, in Mrs. Knee's class, animosity was at a peak for Steve and me. He started shoving me around and challenged me to fight after school. Steve blurted out to the whole class, "Come on punk, I'll beat your face in!"

I accepted the challenge. There was no other option. "No problem, you big puss. I'll kick you're ass!" I answered with a gulp and a tingle of disbelief in my voice.

All day long friends tried to convince me to back down. Bill, or as he was called, "The Animal", came up to me like a big brother would, and said "Clifton, I think you might get your butt kicked." Still, pride is sometimes bigger than common sense.

All day long my concentration was shot. My stomach

felt as if there were a thousand butterflies trying to escape through my throat. Apprehension was at maximum.

Finally, 2:10 P.M. came. As I made my way to my locker, the throngs were gathering. Some good friends said, "Kick his ass," but for the most part I couldn't hear a word anyone was saying. I dumped all my books off in my locker, and quickly walked towards the field. I saw Steve at a distance with a Cheshire cat grin on his face. All his buddies were laughing and snickering.

I didn't say a word, but adrenaline was causing my heart to sound like a kettle drum I could hear from the band room in the distance.

The crowd designated our boxing ring by circling around like a mob of gamblers at a cock fight. Not too many people cared who won, but just the excitement of a good fight drew a crowd. I put my fists up, as did Steve. "SMACK!" went the first punch, as it connected with my face and knocked me to the ground. I bounced back up as if I was on a trampoline. "SMACK" went the next punch as I hit Steve with a right to the chin. It was quite a reach for me as he was much taller. He swung wildly with the same side arm he used as a pitcher. He missed, so I seized the opportunity and clobbered him with a right and a left, getting him more off-balance. I don't remember much else about the fight, except that he didn't connect a punch again, and my fists were sore from nailing him many, many times.

The next thing I remember was two large arms grabbing me around the shoulders. I looked around and there stood Coach Halverson, who was a tough disciplinarian. He was the one who would always quote "When the going gets tough, the tough get going." He lived by this philosophy all the way through the cancer he would succumb to a few years later.

I was ready for him to start yelling at me, but instead he pulled me off to one side and said, "I think you got the best of him, Clifton." No suspension, no laps, no push-ups, no nothing! He must have known a little more about what was going on than I thought.

The next day I could hardly wait to get to school I was a hero — for a while, anyway. Steve was very quiet the next few days. I was lauded as a great fighter. I really didn't think so, but who's to dispute the masses? Instant fame was nothing to argue with.

Well, it's hard to keep a good man down — Steve, that is. Within days after our fight, a Sea World helicopter crashed in Steve's backyard. Both pilots were killed, one by decapitation. On the point system of adolescent popularity, Steve gained twice as many points as he had lost in our fight. Who could compete with bodies strewn all over the backyard?

That was okay, though. I didn't mind being second string, mostly since Bill, "The Animal", had come up to me after the fight and expressed his satisfaction with my kicking Steve's butt. Having approval from him was good enough for me.

Bill had grown up on Black Mountain Boulevard with his younger brother and two younger sisters. His father was a policeman and a tough disciplinarian.

However, the value system of this family was unusual, to say the least. There was a story going around that a married couple up the street couldn't conceive. This was well before artificial insemination, so the next best thing was to find the neighborhood stud and utilize his services. With mutual consent between both couples, the Animal's dad fathered a son by the neighbor so Bill had a half-brother out there somewhere. The modus operandi of the children seemed to be survival of the fittest. It was a perfect nest in which to raise an outlaw, biker, and murderer.

Bill went through different phases, as did the rest of us. There was a period of time that many in our gang turned to a new movement — one that had broken out of the hippie movement — and became known as "Jesus People." This conversion lasted a short while for some, but it changed others for a lifetime. Bill and his brother did turn, if only for a short time, to Christianity.

Bill seemed to be going through a lot of personal problems. The next year, when he was in eleventh grade, he overdosed on Seconals at school, and was taken to juvenile hall where he stayed for the summer. He was being molded into "The Animal" that the newspapers would write about in future years.

There was always a slightly sadistic streak in Bill. One day back in 1970, a few of us were outside of his house. Bill, his brother Steve, Sonny and his sister Vickie and I were just shooting the breeze and smoking a joint. Vickie was very pregnant, and only in the eleventh grade. Bill was joking around and ended up throwing Vickie down on the street. I was shocked, and Vickie was in a panic. Bill apologized, saying he didn't know what had come over him.

I was fifteen when some friends of mine, one of whom was Brad Bening, (brother of the actress Annette Bening), and I were looking for a place to roll some pot into joints. It was rainy outside, so we decided to go to the San Carlos golf course and roll some in the bathroom. Brad and another friend were standing by to warn us outside the bathroom while Terry and I each went into a different stall to roll.

Terry was a short, nearsighted kid who refused to wear glasses. The way he squinted made him look like the character Tweetie Pie, thus earning him that nickname. A month before the golf course incident I was to meet Terry and take some LSD with him. I woke up on a beautiful September morning and took over half of a hit of Orange Sunshine. I watched the sun rise from my front porch and proceeded to hitchhike to Terry's house on the western edge of San Carlos.

There wasn't a cloud in the sky, and Black Mountain appeared majestic and looming as I was coming on to the acid. It took fifteen minutes. The blue sky became a movie screen for the hallucinations I was beginning to experience. I was feeling euphoric and could not remove the grin from my face. Over 200 micrograms of LSD made it very difficult to communicate with the person who had picked me up hitchhiking. I just said thanks and grinned as I left the vehicle.

I made it to Terry's house, and as usual there was a household of kids, eight children in his family alone, not to mention all of their friends. I gave Terry his portion of the acid, and he came on within fifteen minutes also. It was very fresh and very powerful. I was having a great time talking to his parents, and he couldn't understand how I could do this. I guess dealing with insanity at my house on a daily basis helped me deal with the insanity of LSD. I was completely fried at this point. A glance in the bathroom mirror showed me that my pupils were as large as saucers. Terry was acting spooked from the acid, so we left the house.

As we started walking towards the east we noticed the sky was getting darker. The Santa Ana winds from the east were dropping ashes on us. Terry was convinced it was the end of the world. I wasn't sure what was going on. Soon San Carlos was consumed in a dark cloud. The sun was gone and more and more ash was falling from the sky. It was a relief to find out there was an enormous fire in the east county causing the display and not God releasing one of the vials in the book of Revelation. Still, Terry would avoid acid after that day.

That night I had to go to work at El Cajon Speedway selling sodas. I had to strap a whole case of bottles around my neck. It was extremely hard to count change, as stoned as I was.

Through all the hundreds of times I took LSD, I was searching for some peace and fulfillment, besides just getting high. It never happened. Something strange always took place to put a damper on the experience. It made me think that perhaps just because something was "spiritual", it wasn't necessarily from God. This whole scene brought a scripture to mind that I learned as a kid: "God is not the author of confusion."

The next month at the golf course, whiled Terry and I were in the bathroom rolling joints, Brad came rushing in said the code words: "We've got to go, my bike is *busted*!" I knew we were in trouble then. I was trying to flush the pot down the toilet when I heard the voice of an older man yelling "Hey, what are you guys doing in there?" Terry was in the next stall acting like he was throwing up. All in all it must have looked pretty funny. When I looked behind me I saw a face looking under the stall saying "Open this damn door or I'll break it!" Well, Terry chose the latter but I threw the door open. As the pot was trying to escape down the toilet, I ran past the man and tried to escape, but another golfer, a man in his forties, grabbed me and bounced my head against the bathroom wall about ten times. They only got a little pot from my side of the toilet and Terry managed to get his flushed.

Brad and our other friend got away. When the police came and took Terry and me home, my head was bleeding and full of bumps. I told the police I had been assaulted, and they laughed and said, "So what. You are a criminal in the process of a crime."

It wouldn't have been so bad, but when the police got me to my house, my dad dragged me into the car for the punishment of the late sixties and early seventies — a haircut. It wasn't just a trim, but a buzz job! I was in complete humiliation. The barber at the Navy Hospital had a tough time keeping the razor even with all the bumps on my head.

The police had dropped Terry off first, and his mother was in shock, not that Terry was arrested, but that I, the good role model, was sitting in the back of a police car. I knew I would not be getting any dinner invites in the near future.

The police, and then the judge at a later date, said that if I would sign a complaint against the other three, I would get off easier. I didn't have to think for more than five seconds — "NO WAY!"

I felt such a sense of oneness with my friends, "the underground", and any other group that took a stand against the "establishment." On the other hand, I had never before felt such a separation from my parents, especially my dad. I had always felt a distance between my mom and me, but my dad was always supportive. But now that had changed. The date was October 3, 1970.

The following week at school, all the stoners had heard about the big bust. We plotted revenge against the golf course. One friend who worked there was going to leave the golf cart door unlocked. We were planning to come back in the middle of the night, steal the carts, and tear up the greens. Another friend who lived across the street from the golf course was going to get his .22 rifle and blow the windows out of the club house from his back yard. They were all waiting for my go-ahead. At this time I had some fear of authority — though it wouldn't last long. Anyway, I never gave the green light.

It seemed that all of our childhood friends were deciding which side of the fence they wanted to hang out on. For the most part, they would choose the drug culture.

About a year after high school, a bunch of us from San Carlos rented a large house overlooking Highway 8. Sonny, John and some other high school friends, Shaun, Tony, resided there. We had a large pot plantation that the cops eventually busted. Sonny and John, who had both just moved in, took the rap for the plants just because they were the only ones home. There was honor amongst our friends — I had always felt that brotherhood was where it was at. My dog, Coke, and Shaun's dog, Zeb (who looked so much like a Tasmanian Devil that girls who came over thought he was one after we joked about it) were doing their duty of protecting the pot and barked at the cops, until, we were told by Sonny and John, the cops knocked them out. They never said how.

After our house in Allied Gardens got busted, I moved to Lakeside by myself. I moved into a funky two-bedroom duplex on a street called Short. It was a dirt road with a series of duplexes and other styles of farm ghetto architecture. Everyone had dogs, pigs, horses — anything that produced one form of manure or the other.

It wasn't long before the Animal, his younger brother, and Tony moved in. We all had dogs except for the Animal's brother. I had my big white female German Shepherd (named Coke for an obvious reason). The Animal's Doberman Pincher was called Lucifer — a fitting name. Tony's dog, Sadie, looked like a smaller version of my German Shepherd. Not only did we sabotage our own lives, but we dragged our animals into it.

Eventually we got two pigs to add to our mini-zoo. While living there, I got my second drunk-driving arrest, which cost me my driver's license. My life seemed to be going down the tubes quickly now. I started using the needle more than ever — going from cocaine to heroin. We were so hard up that we used new pig needles, which were about three times the size of a normal human needle.

The Animal was always, without fail, engaged in a "mini" war with someone. One time we were driving to a keg party, and some guy and his girlfriend cut us off in his truck. The Animal was furious. We caught up and signaled for them to pull over. This guy was huge and he piled out with hammers in both hands. The Animal said "Put down the hammers and fight like a man." The guy handed his girlfriend the hammers. She then turned to me saying "Don't even try to jump in, or I'll smash your skull." I couldn't believe that this pretty blond was so tough. I was going to jump in anyway if Bill needed help. This big guy was getting some good punches in, until he pulled Bill's hair. The Animal had a tough time growing his hair long. Messing with what he did have was a good way to detonate the dynamite that was ready to go off in the Animal anytime.

"You pulled my hair, you mother f—! I'm going to kill you!" Bill just started to beat the tar out of this guy.

Finally, the big dude succumbed: "Okay, okay, let's call it quits!" I had laid my sunglasses on a parked car. The chick just picked them up and walked off with them and her wounded beau. I felt kind of impotent, but "The Animal" seemed to have everything under control. Our friendship took a slightly different turn after this day. I think he felt I should have jumped in anyway.

Another time after he and his brother and I moved to Santee, which is east of San Carlos, Bill got upset with Tony about something. . Tony was about my size, and very strong, but he was no match for The Animal. Bill planned to beat up Tony over this issue, which I'm sure was minor. There was a keg party in San Carlos, and both Tony and Bill knew each other would be there. I purposely didn't go. Before the keg party, Bill said "Your buddy Tony is going to get his ass kicked tonight." That's when I decided to do something else. Tony was brave to show up to the party. Bill did thrash him, and after that The Animal was no longer upset with him.

Once, my friend Mack came over to our Santee house to party. He was an old San Carlos buddy. It was getting late and Bill worked construction, so he had to get up early. We were making noise in the living room. And Bill came out and asked us to keep it down. Mack was loud and boisterous when drunk, so that was a nearly impossible task. The next thing we knew, The Animal kicked his bedroom door open. Mack went over to Bill and was trying to calm him down. Mack was no small guy. He was a roofer and tough as nails. The Animal cocked his arm-Smash!-Mack was on his back. "Turn out the lights, the party's over." I don't think Mack ever heard the fat lady singing!

At the little house on Short Street, the beginnings of

something bigger were happening to friends of mine. Many of them rode Harley-Davidsons and looked like the typical outlaw bikers. But they were starting to change. One friend we grew up with, called "Hank", was hanging out with the Hell's Angels. But even more interestingly, he was also hanging out with a fairly new outlaw motorcycle club called the Mongols.

Tony had a Sportster, and was building a Knucklehead — a Harley-Davidson with a bigger engine — on my kitchen floor. Tony, though, seemed to always retain his identity. This is probably the reason he never joined the Mongols. He had some foresight.

The Angels and the Mongols engaged in a bloody turf war that cost many lives on both sides. It was a real live war that divided San Diego into one large battle zone for territory and pride. The Hell's Angels ruled the methamphetamine market and were the premier outlaws in the west. The Mongols were the "upstarts" moving in on them, riding with their colors flying in total defiance. In a few short years Bill would be the president of the Mongols, a part which he was cast in during his formative years. It would cause him to take at least one life, and destroy his own.

While I was waging my own personal war, a larger one was already in progress. A lot of my buddies from San Carlos were wearing the colors of the outlaw Mongols. The battle gear was a Harley-Davidson, a gram of crank, and a

.38.

CHAPTER 3

THE WAR OF COLORS

"Happiness is a warm gun, shoot, shoot, bang, bang." The Beatles

The year was 1976. Although my allegiance was to my brothers in San Carlos, I ended up fifteen miles directly west for a season. For the next few years I called Ocean Beach my home.

Ocean Beach was a refuge for those running from the law, drug dealers who needed to blend into the crowd, political activists, and the Hell's Angels. I was living on Muir Street almost directly across from a bar called Lai Lani's. I found myself in there every day drinking with one or more of my buddies. My friend Mack was going through a divorce at this time, so I assisted him in drowning his sorrows. Lai Lani's was also the designated drinking hole for the local chapter of the Hell's Angels.

I partied with such people as "Snake", "Dirt", "Big Schultz", "Little Schultz", and a myriad of others. Only once did I get on the wrong side of them.

There was a big keg party on Cape May Avenue in a duplex. I had ingested some LSD and was pretty stoned with all the beer I had also consumed. I had a crush on a girl named Mandy who was being bothered by a guy whom I knew was "Mexican Mike's" cousin Steve. "Mexican Mike" was a Hell's Angels prospect. A prospect is someone who is trying to get into the organization. I told Steve to leave her alone. He said "Do you want to go outside?" I agreed, and after connecting two punches to his face, the next thing I knew was that I was on the ground getting kicked by six or seven bikers.

I thought I was going to die, so I yelled in defiance "All Angels suck!" One heavy set girl who was my friend had the guts to try pulling these guys off of me. My other friends and my faithful Shepherd Coke just stood by and watched. Since I was under the influence of acid the feelings of my life passing before my eyes were intensified. Another guy grabbed me out of the crowd and pulled me away.

"OB Jim" stood by while many people in the crowd one by one came up to him and told him what I had said. Jim was the Sargent of Arms for the Angels. "Mexican Mike" kept yelling "Let's kill him!" My mind, for some reason, flashed to Jesus. The whole scene reminded me of the crowd yelling out "Crucify Him!" Although, of course, Jesus was innocent and I knew I was guilty.

Survival is our strongest instinct, and at this particular time it was working overtime in me. I told "OB Jim" that I just broke up with my girlfriend, (which was true), that I had lost my job, (which was also true), and that I was stoned out of my mind (very evident). He decided to let me go. Many thoughts passed through my mind. One was that if they knew that some of my closest friends were Mongols, with whom they were at war, I would have certainly died. I was grateful to go home even though my face and head looked like one mass of blood and bumps.

Not long after that, the Animal and "Hank" paid me a visit in Ocean Beach. They were aware of Lai Lani's bar being a Hell's Angels hangout and they wanted me to clue them about the Angels' comings and goings. This was the summer of 1976 and the Mongols were at a peak with the war on the Angels. I did my best to remain neutral in this situation. I had become friends with several Hell's Angels. By now "Mexican Mike", "Snake", "Dirt", "The Hulk", "O.B. Dave", "Little Schulze" and many more drank with me at Lai Lani's, or came over to Mack's house where I was staying to "do lines".

I chose not to get involved and told Bill and Hank I couldn't help them.

Bill always had someone new to be upset with. We used to box in the living room with two pairs of sixteen ounce gloves I had. I was the only guy stupid enough to box Bill. He would tell me to watch how I connected, or he would dust me. One night we were just having wrestling matches in the living room, and I accidentally made Bill bleed. He was drunk, and after wrestling quite a few people, he noticed some blood on his head. He yelled,

"Who made me bleed?", and his brother said that I had. Bill grabbed my left big toe and shoved it in his mouth. He proceeded to bite very hard down to the bone. I thought I would be toeless forever! I tried to be as macho as possible, so I didn't yell, but sure felt like it!

On Easter Sunday of 1975 most of the guys from our house, and some friends from San Carlos decided to play baseball. We had a keg, so we were all pretty smashed by the time it was over. I sat on the hood of Bill's Rambler as he took off. I could hear his crazy laughter as he floored the gas over a speed bump. I smashed my head and hands on the curb after doing an involuntary Superman imitation. I broke one wrist, sprained the other, and suffered a concussion. With a cast on one arm and a sling on the other, I found it difficult to even open a can of food for me or my dog.

"Dirt" was another tough little dude. He was a custodian at Dana Junior High at the same time I was a substitute custodian. He was also a full-fledged member of the Hell's Angels. I remember one night bringing some cocaine to work. I was, at this time, extremely sick with hepatitis but didn't know it-the drugs were killing me. I had anticipated dealing with dirt that night, but not with the Hell's Angel, rather with the stuff on the classroom floors. Anyway, I ran into Dirt, and since we had done a lot of partying together in Ocean Beach where we both lived, (and since he was scamming on my girlfriend Judy), we immediately offered each other some drugs. I gave him a line of coke, and he gave me a large line of crank, or methamphetamine, which was the Hell's Angels drug of choice. I am amazed I lived past this era — I can't remember not being on drugs in those days.

Dirt, whose real name is Ronald Liquori Sr. would later be sentenced to life in prison without the possibility of parole for multiple convictions on narcotics and weapons charges. He was also charged with making methamphetamine and illegal gun possession. While sentencing Dirt, federal judge Judith N. Keep said that he had used violence and threats to control other Hell's Angels members, including one who was severely beaten. She also said that Dirt was an organizer and manager of a drug conspiracy. Dirt's son, "Dust" or Ron Liquori Jr., was sentenced around the same time with similar charges.

Dirt wasn't the only biker headed for hard time. As years progressed, Bill was becoming more of "The Animal" and less Bill. He had found his niche in life. He had answered his calling and clothed himself with the appropriate mantle; as commander-in-chief of an army at war.

In 1976, Ocean Beach still retained qualities that set it apart from most other communities in San Diego. Today, many of the low rent beach shacks that were constructed during the Forties and turned into permanent rentals have been mowed down and replaced with ultra- modern edifices. These appeal to quite a different cliental than that which used to inhabit this area. What could have been called Haight-Ashbury of the Seventies is now the yuppieville of the new century. Some niches of the Sixties still exists as low-rent shanties occupied by the drug-influenced youth. In the Seventies, however, it was like one large family and as in any large family, not everyone got along.

One common denominator was drugs. LSD and methamphetamines were big. The Hell's Angels were the main distributors of the speed. It was not uncommon for fifty lbs. of high-grade Columbian pot to make it through my living room on any given weekend. Cocaine was becoming the drug of choice, and there were some members of this community who were heroin junkies. I got involved with some people buying Quaaludes. There were plenty of doctors who would write prescriptions for these junkies, who would in turn sell the "ludes" for two bucks a piece, then buy their heroin. Somehow or another, we all had a common thread, like a pact made in hell. Some of my buddies from San Carlos were worrying about my adventures into the wonderful world of #26-point needles (used to inject drugs into the blood stream). We shared needles and injected heroin, methamphetamines, cocaine, and barbiturates into our veins. My friends had good reason to worry. Dirt and Bill weren't the only ones among us headed for a hard fall. Mine would be different but just as harsh.

Lai Lani's, on the corner of Abbott Street and Muir Street, and was definitely not in sync with the discos that were the pre-yuppie hangouts of the mid-Seventies. It was a place for the biker elite and their followers. Not only did we sabotage our own lives, but we dragged our animals into it.

One night while I was staying at Mack's, the Lai Lani's lady bartender came running in our front door screaming about some rednecks with guns in the bar, and no one around to help. The Angels were probably out on a run, and since it was Sunday night, the place was fairly empty. No one reverenced Sunday, and most were hung over and burned out from a weekend on nonstop crystal meth and alcohol partying. Well, the brave but stupid tendencies I possessed at times picked me off the couch. Another friend joined me as I was walking to Lai Lani's. Sure enough, two redneck types in their thirties were shooting pool. I could see a gun handle sticking out of the shorter one's belt. It appeared pool wasn't the only thing they wanted to shoot. I spouted off, "What do you guys want around here?"

The taller one retorted, "None of your f----- business."

Before I could say another word, the shorter one pulled out what looked like a sawed-off shotgun. I was wondering how he could play pool with that down his pants. Running like I did when competing in the 100-yard dash in high school, I believe we set some kind of record that night. We jammed up Muir Street in time to hear two shots go off and the shot pellets hitting to our right and left. This confirmed that what had looked like a sawed-off shotgun theory was one. We didn't even get grazed, but my heart was beating a mile a minute. I think Barbara, the bartender, resorted to what was the last resort — calling the police. I don't know what happened to those guys, but thoughts of the shortness of life ran through my mind again.

A good friend of mine named Bob also stayed at Mack's house while he was on leave from the Navy. Bob was originally from Wisconsin. He was a tall, good-looking, bearded man who enjoyed sports. I taught him how to surf, and we spent many days catching waves just down from Mack's house in O.B. Bob liked to get stoned, but he was intelligent enough to stay away from some of the heavier things. One drug he didn't stay away from, but should have, was LSD.

On September 24, 1978, he definitely should have. It was Sunday night in Ocean Beach. My guitar teacher, Balzi, who also was the leader of a local band, had gotten some strong LSD. It was called windowpayne, the sister of clearlite. Bob and I took some windowpayne, and Bob reacted much differently than he had previously on LSD. He started getting paranoid. He thought one of the guys we were partying with was a homosexual who was hitting on him. He was wrong on both counts. After Bob and I went back to Mack's house, I got him calmed down somewhat. We drank a few beers, but Bob was still a little strange. The next morning Bob and I were still high from the LSD. It was a beautiful day; there was a high-pressure system causing clear blue skies and hot, dry temperatures. This is better known as a Santa Ana condition. Bob and I walked down to the beach. On the way back we noticed a large cloud of smoke interrupting the gorgeous blue horizon. Our first thought was that there was a large fire, so we went back to the pad and turned on the radio. At 9:02 that morning a Pacific Southwest Airlines jetliner and a small plane had collided over North Park in San Diego. It was the worst air disaster in U.S. history at that point. Everyone on both planes was killed, as well as people in some houses below.

This affected me deeply, but not as deeply as it touched Bob. He thought that there was some conspiracy. He completely flipped out. We got him back to the Navy base in Long Beach, where he was admitted to the hospital and was eventually diagnosed as schizophrenic.

Back in 1976, my former roommate Tony, his girlfriend Sue, Marty and his girlfriend, Annette Bening, and my girlfriend Judi, and I were having a campfire off Voltaire Street in Ocean Beach. We were drinking beers, smoking pot, and getting somewhat stoned. Someone dared me to walk across the board that was burning in the fire for a beer. I was barefooted. I'm amazed how stupid one can be when intoxicated. It seemed like an easy thing to do, so I tried it. About half-way across, the board broke-CRACK!

Needless to say, I fell in the fire, and my right foot got cooked. All six of us went on top of Ocean Beach pier and I cooled my foot in the fish wash tank. Every pump of blood brought intense pain. The following week, I took a bus to the doctor, since I had lost my license for drunk driving a couple of years earlier. I was eligible to get it back but I couldn't afford insurance nor could I afford a car. The doctor was so amazed at how badly burned my foot was that he took slides of it for a class he was teaching.

The following days weren't much better. My girlfriend dumped me, and I lost my job doing lapidary work, which in simple terms is jewelry making, using motorized wheels to grind stones into the shape you desire. The guy I worked for paid me $2.15 per hour. This was under minimum wage, and he got away with it because he told me, even after three months on the job, that I was still "in training".

I also got kicked out of the place where I was living. The owner didn't like my dog. To top this off, I came down with scabies. Scabies are microscopic parasites that suck your blood. The condition can be spread by touch. My dog even got them and it was nearly impossible to get rid of them with all that fur hiding the infected skin. I had to wash my dog, treat her with lotion, wash my clothes, then wash myself and finally, apply Kwell lotion to my skin. If you missed one scabie, it would multiply when itched and the process had to start over. My vet told me to put my dog to sleep because of how hard it was to cure. I couldn't do that. Eventually we got better.

I was homeless, jobless, girlfriendless, couldn't walk very well, and was battling a two-front war on scabies. It was not one of my better years. Finally some old friends with whom I had roomed before allowed me to sleep on their porch at first, then on their floor. My dog was with me, of course. These two friends were from New Jersey, and were characters. Ollie's family was from Finland, and Pete was third generation New Jersey native. Ollie and I eventually went into the gardening/landscape business together after we were fired working as gardeners for a large property management company. We were due for a pay raise, but I think they were mad at us for using the Jacuzzi and weights after work. Pete worked as little as possible, and scammed where he could. Anyway, I was grateful for Ollie and Pete.

I was still very much in touch with San Carlos and my friends. Marty, Shaun, and I got together on a regular basis. Before Marty was going with Annette, we spent many days and nights in a blurred reality.

One night Marty and I had a Mezcal guzzling contest. We both drank a quart of this Mexican poison that is derived from a cactus, like tequila, except more powerful.

In Mezcal there is a worm at the bottom that has a large concentration of the active ingredients and is rumored to cause hallucinations when consumed. But who could tell after drinking a bottle of this stuff? All I remember was a little bit of the party we were at, and puking my guts out all night as well as bouncing off the walls with Marty.

Marty was a tall, strong, mountain man with a weathered face. He never had any problems finding beautiful girlfriends. Besides Annette Bening, he once dated a pin-up girl from a popular adult magazine.

When we were both nineteen we had tried to find a graduation party in San Carlos that was supposed to be near the high school. It was June of 1974. We both took some reds, better known as Seconal, and didn't seem to be getting stoned. We drank some whiskey to speed things up, and Marty was beginning to weave his little Metro all over Navajo Road. I told Marty that I should drive, since I was under control, or so I thought. About 100 feet after I took over the wheel, "SMASH!" The Metro ended up on a curb next to Patrick Henry High School. I ruined the A-frame of my friend's car. We got out of the car, drank some more Jack Daniels, and began to walk up the street. Marty and I decided to have a friendly wrestling match on someone's front yard. The people of the house came out, and I thought they were friendly enough. They ended up calling the police. Later we found out the lady of the house worked for the District Attorney's office.

Marty and I were both passed out on the lawn when the police arrived. I remember opening my eyes and looking over at Marty. He seemed to open his eyes at the same time. "Let's split. The cops!" Marty yelled in his inebriated voice. I got up and started running, but I was heavily sedated by drugs and alcohol. One of the officers ran me down and tackled me. Marty was handcuffed and started kicking the cop and yelling "Stop beating on my friend, you chickenshit pig!"

Marty had a brown belt in karate, and it took both policemen to restrain him. They ended up slamming Marty and me against the police car. I yelled at one of them with conviction, "If I didn't have these cuffs on, I'd beat your ass."

The next thing I knew, Marty and I were being thrown in the back of the police car. Then for some reason, the cops walked away. Marty was holding reds, I was holding weed. We were both handcuffed, but we managed to assist each other in stashing the lid and Seconals under seat directly in front of us. "I hope they don't find this. We're up the creek if they do," I whispered.

We finally arrived at the police station holding tank below the jail in downtown San Diego. The officer that I had challenged uncuffed me and said, "Okay punk, now's your chance. Go ahead and hit me!" I declined. Once in a great while, I came to my senses. But not for long.

While inside the police station, the sheriffs deputies

make you strip for a thorough search. You have to spread your "cheeks" and face the deputy who is searching you. I made the mistake of being a smart punk. "I bet you really enjoy your job," I said to him as I was spread-eagle. He didn't take to this lightly. He replied, "What was that?" I repeated what I said, and before I could finish the sentence, "POP!" He nailed me in the jaw with a left hook. I turned around and clenched my fists. He calmly said, "Unclench your fists." I obliged, and he decked me. Then, he and three other deputies dragged me off to the "rubber room". The rubber room was about 5' by 5' square with concrete walls. I still don't know why they call it the rubber room. There was only a tiny window in the door, and a hole in the middle of the room for relieving one's self. Cockroaches were my only company. I was in there naked in these filthy conditions for a couple of hours. I kept my mouth shut because I could overhear a guy in the next room yelling and cursing. He got the attention of the deputies, alright, if that was his goal. I could hear him getting beaten. At this point, I realized that "Silence is truly golden." I was eventually released and put into the holding tank with the rest of the criminals. I was surprised to see my friends Sonny and John in there. They were busted for being drunk in public and possession of a small amount of pot. Marty, John, Sonny and I looked out for each other that weekend in jail, and were all released in forty-eight hours on our own recognizance. Marty and I were charged with malicious mischief. The "drunk in public" and "challenging an officer" charges were dropped. Also, we were never charged with possession of the drugs we stashed in the cop car. I couldn't for the life of me imagine that they weren't ever found. Nevertheless, 1 didn't argue with them about it.

Soon after Bill the Animal and "Hank" visited me, I heard on the news, as well as along the grapevine, that 'Hank" and "Red Beard," who was a Mongol, had been riding their hogs along a secluded road in east county, when a van pulled alongside the road opened the doors, and heavy artillery shattered the silence with the sputtering of automatic weapons. "Red Beard" was killed. But fortunately "Hank" escaped injury. To this day, there is a lot of mystery as to how the Hell's Angels knew those two would be riding along that road at that time.

I was living with Animal, his brother Steve, and Sonny and John in Santee. Brock and Ron, (not Liquori), both soon-to-be-Mongols, were harbored from the police at our house when there was a warrant for their arrest for destroying a Jack-In-The-Box.

I was on the phone with my buddy Shaun and remember saying nonchalantly, "Oh, I've got to go. The sheriffs have surrounded the house." When they took Ron and Brock away, Steve said "Oh look. I've got dibs on Brock's coat." Brock had left his Levi jacket during the futile attempt to ditch the cops.

The Animal heard him say this, and I can still see the eyes of a mad bull in him. Bill pulled his Buck and Rigid knives out and proceeded to stab his brother in both of his sides. Steve picked Bill up, which was a feat in itself because since Bill was much bigger than him. It was an unusual site: Bill was stabbing him while being held up in the air. Then Steve abruptly dropped his brother and ran outside with Bill in hot pursuit. Bill got to his car and tried to run over his bro. Steve made it back a couple of days later good as new. No hard feelings.

Anyway, Brock and Ron were beginning to hang out with the Mongols, and by 1976, they were members. I heard that Brock's girlfriend answered a knock at their door and got her head blown off in the process. The war went on.

What makes someone a murderer? I knew there was a soft spot in Bill, but it was becoming more and more difficult to find. He had a reputation to protect. He was the "Animal". As president of the Mongols in Southern California, he was at war and had to lead his troops into battle. He was a rebel with a cause — his only response to the attacks on his "brothers" was retaliation.

On January 16, 1982, Bill and some other Mongols met with a Mongol named Leonard at his house in Santee. Bill waved a silver .38 caliber revolver and said, "Let's go kill a f------ Hell's Angel!" Then they discussed whose car to take.

Gang members Leonard, Bruce, and Doug left the house together. Scott Michael joined them, and they arrived at The Horseshoe Tavern around 1:00 A.M. January 17. Raymond Piltz, a member of the Hell's Angels Motorcycle Club, was by himself. All of the Mongols attacked him, and it is believed that Scott Michael shot him. After this, Bill hit Piltz with a table; then everyone split. Soon, they met at the current Mongol President's house, but Doug and Scott went elsewhere.

Bill fled the city and changed his identity, until for whatever reason, he turned himself in. At the time, Bill was married to Valerie, a pretty blonde who didn't seem to fit into his present lifestyle. She was a country girl who enjoyed riding her horses. Before they were married, she had left in 1975 and had begun a relationship with someone else. I was living with Bill at the time, and had never seen him so melancholy. It didn't stop him from going out on her, though. Eventually, they got back together and Valerie beat up on of the girls Bill was seeing when she was gone. By 1982, they had a son, and another baby on the way.

Many letters went to the Honorable William T. Low, the judge presiding over Bill's case. One such letter from Bill's parents blamed the Mongol's influence for their son's behavior. They feared Bill would be harmed by other gang members if he were imprisoned. There was a war going on

, and there would have been nothing worse than sticking one prisoner of war in with the opposing side.

They also mentioned the adversity Bill had overcoming his speech impediment while growing up. Bill's parents pleaded for mercy for Bill's children's sake. They offered to help out Bill when he got out. Bill also wrote a letter to the judge that put things into focus. He did blame his association with the Mongols for many of his problems, but he did own up to being partly responsible for Piltz's murder. The letter started out in a very wordy fashion.

"Being a citizen of one of the few countries in the world that allows you the opportunity to choose the path of your own destiny, I cannot find in my heart any excuses for the crime of which I have pleaded guilty to, but only to express reflections of my thoughts on this tragic event that has marred not only my life, but as well the lives of my family and loved ones, along with the lives of people I will never know."

Bill ended the letter by saying; "I feel that I owe it to my family and to myself to change my life for the better and to make myself a useful and respected part of society, and with the determination and God's help I know I will."

I don't know if Bill has changed, but time will tell how much sincerity there was in his letter. Bill has since been released from prison, and I talked to one of his siblings about him last year. He said that Bill was still in trouble with the law, but they were seeking medical help for him, in case there was something psychologically wrong with him, causing his violent temper.

The black cloud of murder seemed to enjoy its stay on Black Mountain Boulevard.

CHAPTER 4

CREATION OF A PSYCHOPATH; THE DAVID ALLEN LUCAS STORY

"Rape, Murder, it's just a shot away." The Rolling Stones

I remember walking to school one fall morning and seeing two friends riding up on bikes as fast as they could. It was 1967, and I had recently met Jon Jackson and David Allen Lucas. Jon lived on Ballenger, and Dave lived on Black Mountain Boulevard, which was the next block over. Jon was a stocky kid with black hair and a friendly smile. Dave was a lanky kid with a sandy complexion and blond hair. His teeth were slightly bucked giving him a kind of "hillbilly" appearance. They both were on their fake Sting-Ray bikes, had wide grins on their faces, and seemed to be out of breath as if they were in a race. Well, they were racing to beat out any spectators that might have seen them torch a mailbox a couple of blocks away. Since I was trying to establish friendships with them, I just said something to the effect of "Bitchin', man!" as they were explaining the details to me. In all of my twelve years, the closest I had come to doing something like that was when I lit fire in a trash can in the bathroom at Cleveland Elementary. A boy named Bruce was with me.

Bruce was a troubled kid. All the parents in our neighborhood (Lake Ariana Drive) kept saying that "One of these days that kid is going to end up killing somebody." When we were just three years old, he had shown me how to make fire with matches. I also vividly remember his two older brothers and Bruce creating a launcher out of two-by-fours, and shooting large rocks at people from their front yard. They were a rowdy bunch. Their mother seemed to be the only disciplinarian, since their father was a recluse.

The first person to knock the wind out of me was Bruce. I was five years old and wanted to join the big kids in a street football game. Bobby, Bruce's oldest brother, told Bruce to punch me, which he did. We were the same age, and although my nickname was "Butch", Bruce was much tougher than I was. He wound up his stocky little arm, and punched me in the gut as hard as he could. I was lying in the street for a long time until I went whimpering into the house. For years I had fantasies about blowing their house up.

Bruce was also a compulsive liar. Aware at an early age that he was at a disadvantage because of his family's poverty, he made is own reality. There was always yelling and screaming coming out of their house. When the drug culture hit, every one of Bruce's siblings got caught up in it. Except for Bobby. He turned out to be my little league coach, and we were friends. Bruce and I hung out from time to time. We started smoking cigarettes in the sixth grade. When we were in seventh grade, Bruce turned me on to my first drug — speed. I was up all night with my heart racing. I was in love with chemicals from that day forward until I stopped at age twenty-four with some real big assistance.

Anyway, Bruce and I got nailed for lighting the trash can on fire at school. My sixth grade teacher was disappointed in me — an A student who seemed to be going wrong. (One day while going to recess I had taken a shortcut through a special education classroom disturbing everyone. Mr. Woodburn, my teacher, grabbed me by the neck and said "You are really becoming a bad egg".) He couldn't have understood the identity crisis I was going through at the time. Though I know there is no valid excuse for my bad behavior, there were some reasons. My mother was getting progressively more manic-depressive, and I would lie awake at night in turmoil listening to her valium and alcohol induced rampages in which she would accuse my dad and me of anything and everything. The message I got was that I was worthless. My only comfort was my transistor radio playing the top thirty hits on stations KCBQ and KGB. I was a perpetual emotional wreck. What I understand was my deep desire to be totally accepted and loved. Instead, I always felt that the eyes of disdain would follow me out of my house until I found the refuge of my friends. Bruce was one of those friends from time to time. Even though he was hated by most of the adults and many kids, he would reach out to other undesirables and befriend them. Bruce had empathy and compassion, something that was never extended to him.

I got spanked with a belt when my dad got home that night. The fire department even visited my house. Bruce got in trouble too, but he never told the authorities that I was the one who set the fire. Bruce had some depth and loyalty to him.

Less than ten years later Bruce was sentenced in Texas for the murder of a man. Around that time, Bruce's father was arrested for sexually molesting a young girl. I don't know all the details, but I often wonder, in Bruce's case, if his actions were not a self-fulfilling prophesy that might have been instilled in him at an early age. The neighbors, Bruce's and mine, always said that he was crazy enough to kill someone. Perhaps things might have been different if an adult had reached out to him in his youth.

Well, back to Jon and Dave. They were arrested for torching the mail box, which was a federal offence, of course. Jon came back to school after a few days of suspension with his head shaved. What a punishment when long hair was cool. I don't know what the repercussions were for Dave, if any.

As I got to know both guys more through the years, I found that Jon's parents were strong disciplinarians, but David's parents always seemed to be at work. Jon had two younger brothers. David had an older sister and a younger brother. I remember going over to David's house to smoke pot on the mountain behind his house (the afore mentioned Black Mountain). We were going to play some football afterwards with some of the gang: The "Animal", his brother Steve, and our friend Sonny and his brother. It was never difficult to find fifteen guys who wanted to play. On this particular day David was giving his sister a hard time. She was screaming at him: "Keep your hands off of me!" Word was around that David regularly manhandled her. David was nice to his friends, but all along there was a sadistic, perverted side to him.

During 1973, our senior year, David abducted a young woman, raped her, and used a knife to cut her throat and hands. She survived and David was sentenced to four years in the California Youth Authority. After that incident I lost track of David Allen Lucas. Because of his conviction, he missed out on graduating with the rest of us in the Patrick Henry High's class of 1973.

David was a very nice guy on the outside, but was a rabid wolf on the inside. Sandi was a girl who dated David. Here is her story:

"I met David on July 5, 1979. He was at a mutual friend's house, and had just gotten out of a Colorado jail on drug charges a couple of days prior to that, or so he said. Marty and Paul were two people we both had known. David seemed very intelligent, and things just clicked with us. I have a degree in psychology. We both could communicate well about many things we had in common. Dave was a real 'people' person."

Sandi said things began to go sour after a couple of months. "A black person came over to my house to visit, and Dave just happened to be over. After the man left, Dave warned me to never have a 'nigger' over to my house again. Dave seemed threatened by a lot of things. Also, he would disappear for long periods of time, and fail to communicate with me about things. I'm sure there were other girls and drugs involved, although he didn't do drugs around me. He got very angry over things. One day he decided that it was time for us to move in together. I didn't want to, because I had other interests. He was angry about this, and our relationship ended soon after." It appears that David was living a dual existence even at this time.

In the east county of San Diego between 1979 and 1984 there was a one-man reign of terror. Three young ladies and a toddler were brutally murdered, after the women were sexually assaulted. All had their throats cut. A fifth victim was assaulted and left for dead. Fortunately for her and perhaps countless other future victims — she lived. She identified David Allen Lucas as the one who tried to kill her. Lucas has been convicted of three counts of murder.

David had his own carpet cleaning business, and made

his entry into these womens houses through the guise of his business. I had talked to David in the late 70's and he seemed to be getting his life together with his business after being incarcerated for his first sexual conviction.

Lucas was accused of six murders. He was convicted of first-degree murder in the 1979 deaths of Suzanne Jacobs and her three-year-old, Colin, and also for the 1984 death of Catherine Swanke. The Jacobs were found with their throats slashed in their San Diego residence. Swanke, a San Diego State University student, was found on a remote hillside in Spring Valley with her throat slashed. Lucas was convicted of attempted murder of Jody Santiago Robertson of Seattle. She survived the June 9, 1984 attack in which she was brutally choked and had her throat slashed. Kidnapping charges were also added. Robertson testified for the prosecution and for Swanke. Lucas was acquitted in the throat slashing of Gayle Roberta Garcia, a realtor found dead in a vacant Spring Valley house December 8, 1981. The jurors were deadlocked on the murder of Roberta Strang, age twenty-four, and Amber Fisher, age three. Both had their throats slashed when Rhonda was baby-sitting Amber on October 23, 1984. Eleven jurors voted for conviction and one for acquittal.

I wonder why Lucas was ever released after the first offense. I also wonder how close Sandi came to being one of the victims.

Again, several questions arise; how could someone who was a "nice guy" to his friends turn into such a calloused, heartless killer? Also, why did so many people in such a small proximity of suburban America share the same destiny — staggering violence?

Most of them abused drugs, had turbulent family situations, were average to below average students, and had no spiritual background. Many of these people were friends with each other.

But those common denominators don't begin to tell the whole story.

The black cloud had succeeded in smothering the conscience and heart of another of its victims. Unfortunately, this storm is not satisfied with wreaking destruction on one or two, but desires to darken the very souls of an ever-growing number of prey.

CHAPTER 5

A FALLEN EAGLE

"Come on baby, light my fire, try to set the night on fire!"
The Doors

Nancy Alstadt was a quiet girl. I remember her in most
of my classes in junior high. She was an above- average
student. We both used to ace most of the tests in English
and math. She was studious, conservative in dress and
mannerisms, and never invited to parties. She had a
graceful beauty, though it was concealed by her old-
fashioned glasses that helped promote her alienation from
mainstream peer pressure. She had very few friends, but
she didn't seem to mind. Nancy seemed to have a quiet,
patient hope that superseded the immediate. Nancy was
the kind of girl who would be most likely forgotten by the
movers and shakers of the school.

I remember hearing that Nancy was engaged to a guy
named Craig whom I had known since grade school, but
who was a year older. I was happy for them both, although
my circle of friends did not hang out with this group. They
were both very nice people. Then, in 1975, the news came
that further shocked and already turbulent neighborhood.

There was a fire at the Altstadt house. When the fire
was out, what was found inside is was almost too terrible

to describe. Nancy and her parents were found inside hacked to death. Her youngest brother had also been attacked, but he survived. Whoever the attacker was, he tried to use fire to conceal this horrendous crime.

When the truth came out, the intruder, murderer, and arsonist was Danny Altstadt, an Eagle Scout, honor student, and football player at Patrick Henry High School. Beth Polson, a writer for the *San Diego Evening Tribune of* February 22, 1975 reported:

An 18-year-old youth was arrested early today in connection with the killing of his parents and sister and attempted killing of his brother. Dan Altstadt, an Eagle Scout and a straight-A student, is in custody of the San Diego Police Department. Police Lt. Ed Stevens said simply, "We have enough evidence to book him." A Boy Scout axe was recovered as the weapon in the killings, police said. The killings occurred in the family home in San Carlos shortly before 1:30 a.m. today, police estimated. The house at Lake Ben Ave., was sealed off as investigations continue. A fire, which police said began after the killings, heavily damaged a hall and the two front bedrooms where the bodies were found.

The body of William Altstadt, in his early 40's, a systems engineer with Convair, was discovered lying alongside the bed in the master bedroom. The body of the mother, Maxine, a part-time bookkeeper with Wickes Furniture in El Cajon, was found in the bed.

Police said both had been badly beaten. Full reports on the cause of death are pending a coroner's report.

Nancy Altstadt, the 20-year-old sister, who was to have been married this summer, was found on the floor in her bedroom, where the fire apparently started. Her body was burned too severely for police to immediately determine cause of death, Stevens said.

The fifth family member, Gary, 15, is in critical condition at Alvarado Hospital with massive head injuries. "Some of his fingers were cut off," Stevens said.

A neighbor, who asked not to be identified, helped another neighbor pull Gary from the smoke-filled entrance hall before firemen arrived.

As a neighborhood recalled, "Gary mumbled something about 'the man', but he was almost out. According to Stevens, the boy gave a statement to police.

The neighbor said he was awakened around 1:30 a.m. when a girl beat on his door and said the Altstadt house was on fire. His wife called the fire department and the first unit arrived in three minutes, bringing the fire under control in 45 minutes.

Dan arrived at the scene shortly after the fire engines. Neighbors saw him walk around the corner and up to the house. A girl who accompanied him left and no one knew who she was or remembered ever having seen her before.

"He looked like he was in shock", a neighbor said. "He didn't cry... ."

Dan told the police he had walked home from a neighborhood party. He was taken into custody at the scene, according to Stevens.

Routine chemical tests for drugs were administered to the youth but no reports were available on the outcome.

Neighbors who knew "Danny" Altstadt described him as quiet. He had been accepted at UCLA and had planned to begin classes this fall. "He was a handsome boy, the best looking of the three children," a neighbor said. "He was a bright boy, too.

"I was talking to his mother on Monday and she said she had been having some problems with the boy, particularly when Bill was out of town.

"But Danny was the kind of boy I would have completely trusted. They were a super good family and Bill and Maxine were excellent parents...lovely people.

"Bill was a fastidious kind of person. His standards were high... ."

The Altstadt dog, Frisky, lay dead on the driveway today, covered by a boy's jacket. The dog's head was split open.

A white 1974 Courier truck missing from the family garage was found around 9:00 a.m. on Delta St. about 1/2 mile from the killings.

Craig Lapp, a 20-year-old fiancé of Nancy Altstadt, was one of the first people to see Dan when he arrived at the house this morning. "He was real quiet, didn't say a word,"

Craig said.

Dan made no attempt to enter the house and asked no questions about what happened. He appeared weak and Craig helped him to a car to sit down.

A basketball goal was attached to the front of the garage and neighbors saw the Altstadt boys and other neighborhood youngsters playing basketball late yesterday afternoon.

The Altstadts had lived in the San Carlos house about 15 years.

William Altstadt held a master's degree from San Diego State University. The family moved here from Colorado, where Nancy and Dan were born.

The two boys attended Patrick Henry High School where Dan was a member of the football team.

Nancy was a student at Mesa College and worked part-time at a department store. She attended a bridal shower early last night.

The neighbor who reported the fire said the front door and kitchen were locked when he tried to enter the house.

He and another neighbor kicked the door down and found Gary. Gary was given artificial respiration and taken to the hospital.

Another article from the *San Diego Union,* dated February 23, 1975, entitled "Neighbors Say Altstadts 'Were Perfect Family'", quoted neighbors who described the Altstadts as hardworking, good-looking, athletic, helpful, quiet, intelligent, and 'they liked to do stuff together.'" Later on the article states, "Regarding Dan, neighbors said he is the kind of person one uses as an example; he never gives anybody any problems. In fact, he doesn't even drink or smoke.'"

Another article, entitled "Coach Comments", reported:

One of Dan's football coaches, Walt Baranski, said the youngster never gave anyone any problems. He was a defensive lineman who was proud to be part of the team.

Mike Robbins, 16, a Henry sophomore, said his friend Dan, who had a straight A average through most of high school, 'was starting to know more people this year with his football involvement and all.'

Neighbors and classmates said Dan occasionally was grounded. "But this was minor stuff and all the Altstadts held each other in high regard," said a housewife on the block. "It's going to be hard not picturing them going around together anymore."

The article also stated that the garage was full of sports paraphernalia such as golf clubs, surfboards, scuba gear. "Everything is so neat it is hard to believe this kind of thing could happen here," was one comment.

Edwin C. Miller, who was the San Diego District Attorney at the time of the massacre, had some ideas. He wrote an article for the *Evening Tribune,* April 17, 1975, entitled "Violence in the Living Room." Here is the article in its entirety:

The subject of television violence came very close for me only a few weeks ago. A San Carlos couple and their oldest daughter were killed in their home. Their youngest son was nearly killed and their house was set on fire. Our office has since charged their eldest son, an 18-year-old, with those deaths. I am not here to comment on the merits of the case. The determination will be made by a jury in a court of law.

However, there is a coincidence here, one I want to bring to your attention, one you should be aware of.

Less than two weeks prior to the homicides, a national television network broadcast a dramatic program which contained excellent acting by Elizabeth Montgomery. It was a dramatization of the story of Lizzie Borden.

Remember Lizzie Borden? "Lizzie Borden took an axe and gave her mother 40 whacks, and when she saw what she had done, she gave her father 41."

The couple in San Carlos was chopped to death with an axe. There may be nothing here but pure coincidence. But the question must be asked: "Did the program have anything to do with the deaths of three people?" It is a question not easily answered, and perhaps one that will never be answered.

But the circumstantial evidence which is currently tainting television is something I would like you to consider.

Most of you, I'm sure, have read about the so-called "Slasher" killings in Los Angeles. But did you know the killings began the week after a drama depicting similar slayings was aired during a segment of NBC's "Police Story"?

There too the question is raised with respect to the possible connection between television violence and the commission of actual crimes.

In both the San Carlos killings and the "Slasher" slayings, the contention that a relationship exists between the portrayal on the television screen and the actual deaths is mere speculation.

In the current edition of *Ladies Home Journal*, however, the suspicious relationship moves closer to fact. The magazine recounts, for example, the reaction in Boston to a television movie depicting a group of youths dousing a derelict with gasoline and setting him afire for kicks.

The very next day a woman was burned to death in that city, turned into a human torch under almost identical circumstances. That film showed the kids being caught. They were also caught in Boston.

The youngsters admitted getting the idea from what they saw on television.

Several months ago NBC television presented an early evening made-for-television film during prime-time viewing hours. The film was entitled "Born Innocent". You may have seen it.

If you did you know the film showed in explicit fashion the sexual violation of a young girl with a broom handle wielded by female inmates in a juvenile detention home.

Shortly thereafter a California woman sued NBC and its affiliate television in San Francisco, KRON, for $11 million.

The lawsuit charged that this movie had inspired three girls, ages ten, thirteen, and fifteen to commit a similar attack on the woman's nine-year-old daughter and an eight-year-old friend three days after the film aired. Unbelievable? Perhaps. Again, a court of law will have to decide.

The *Ladies Home Journal* goes on to outline two more incidents, which I want to bring to your attention.

A fourteen-year-old boy, after watching rock star Alice Cooper engage in a mock hanging on television, attempted to reproduce the stunt and killed himself in the process.

Another boy laced the family dinner with ground glass after seeing how it was done on a television crime show. That is in fact, not coincidence.

Not so many years ago, Rod Serling wrote a book called *Hijacked*. It told of a pressure bomb being placed on a airline. The extortionist then placed telephone calls to the airline's headquarters saying if the plane reached a certain altitude, it would explode. He wouldn't tell what the altitude was and ransom for the information was paid.

The book, the movie, and the television fare of the same name were extremely successful. Surely it was to be expected that other demented minds would try the same format. They did. Remember a man by the name of D.B. Cooper?

Cooper was the name used by the first person to hijack an airplane and request parachutes. He was apparently successful. Others attempted and were not successful.

However, the legend of Mr. Cooper attached itself to the minds of those who wanted to make a quick buck. And the legend grew with the help of television crews and newspapers and magazine reporters. The fact that no other would-be hijackers using the same demands have succeeded seems to have counteracted the original in-depth reporting of Cooper's apparent success.

We all agree, I hope, that we as Americans do have and should have the right to free expression and the right to a free press. I don't challenge that. Today I am not even calling for official restraints.

I am saying, however, with the well-documented incidences of how television, film, and media violence can cause anti-social behavior by some people in this country, that you need to be aware of what is being shown and printed by the media.

I am not sure that self-restraint is currently being applied by members of the Fourth Estate. I'm afraid numbers, ratings, and ad sales have placed dollar signs ahead of ethics and responsibility. Regardless of my personal opinion, television broadcasters can no longer plead that they are unaware of the potential adverse effects of such programs as "Born Innocent".

During the last decade, two national violence commissions and an overwhelming number of scientific studies have continually come to one conclusion — televised and film violence can powerfully teach, suggest, and even legitimatize extreme anti-social behavior and can, in some viewers, trigger specific aggressive or violent behavior.

A major theme that many television studios have shown repeatedly is that violence is acceptable if the victim "deserved it". This, of course, is a very dangerous and insidious philosophy.

It suggests that aggression, while reprehensible in criminals, is acceptable for the good guys who have every right on their side.

But, of course, nearly every person feels he or she is right, and often the good guys are criminals, whom the film happens to depict sympathetically, as in *The Godfather*. Who is good and who is bad depends on whose side you are on.

And criminals are too frequently shown on television as daring heroes. In the eyes of many young viewers these criminals possess all that's worth having in life — fast cars, beautiful admiring women, super-potent guns, modish clothes, etc. In the end they may die like heroes, almost as martyrs, then only to appease the moralists who insist on crime-does-not-pay endings.

Perhaps I am over-anxious about the relationship of violence on television to violence in our society.

But let me ask you something. If only one per cent of the possible 40 million people saw Lizzie Borden's axe killings on television were stimulated to commit an aggressive act, wouldn't this country have 40,000 additional crimes?

Ed Miller must be aghast at how the violence in San Diego has grown exponentially since the time of his article. A while ago I listened to the president of NBC attempt to explain why there was so much violence on the network he represented. His excuse was that it only reflected society, but did not mold it. It seems like almost an uncontrollable monster is turned loose through the television each night.

It does reflect a small part of society, but generally the worst part. Unfortunately for the viewers who aren't mature enough to differentiate reality from make-believe, they accept this as the norm. Now the monster has more room to grow and can manipulate our society by adjusting the value system at a whim.

Regarding Danny Altstadt, the rumor mill was

immediately at work. Some say he was slipped LSD at a party, and flipped out. Many other things were said, including that Danny was responding to a lot of pent-up anger at a very controlling and domineering father and one night he just couldn't take it any longer. This is all conjecture, and perhaps we will never know why this tragedy happened. The psychologist who has cared for Danny for the past ten years says that he doesn't remember the incident at all.

Note: Since the first writing of the first edition of this book, social media has exploded with the advent of the internet. Along with the good, the bad has kept pace, with pornography, violence, and even terrorism.

I recently interviewed a former friend and neighbor of the Altstadt family. He was two years younger than Danny, but hung out with him from time to time. I'll call him "Bert".

Bert and his family lived on Lake Ben Drive across the street and down from the Altstadts. Bert said there was another side to Danny. A side that gives a different perspective. A side completely different from the "all-American Eagle Scout". Bert said that Danny was always "stuck on himself".

Danny always had his routine chores to do. And, when he borrowed the family truck, he had to keep track of the mileage to turn in to his dad.

Bert said that there was also a sadistic side to Danny.

Bert's sister was an object of harassment by the neighbor kids because of her weight problem. Bert said that he believes Danny was a major player in this haranguing. One summer a group of kids hoisted a dummy up on a light post by Bert's house. The dummy had "porker" written on it. One time Danny threw a large lizard at Bert's sister, and seemed to enjoy the agony she experienced. Another time Danny threw orange paint all over Bert's dad's 1960 Ford pickup.

When Bert and Danny were getting along, they would play ping pong together. When Bert would beat him, Danny would explode. Bert said that Danny never liked to lose at anything. He wasn't exactly the "perfect kid" that he appeared to everyone else.

To date, Danny is still locked up and under care. It was another bizarre and unfathomable turn of events for the San Carlos community.

The cloud again had hovered, loomed, and smothered. The winds of confusion, anger, and rage had blown reason out of existence. In its path lay total destruction. Only a couple of blocks to the east, and a few years down the road, it would find a new resting place.

CHAPTER 6

LIFE IN THE MADHOUSE

"I want to go crazy, crazy on you." Heart

I was still living in Ocean Beach with two fellow drug dealers and needle users. The year was 1978.

One of my housemates was Pat, a strange fellow, very Irish like myself, but deeply into the occultic part of Ireland's history. He drew a pentagram on our wall, without my permission, of course, and was involved with very mysterious and dark practices. Although he was a nice guy, there was a part of Pat that no one could know.

Lee, the other one of my housemates, was a Jewish kid with long blond hair and blue eyes. He was one of the smartest and quickest businessmen I've ever seen. Unfortunately, he would also sell a roommate's possessions to the highest bidder. He stole his best friend's girlfriend right in front of my eyes — integrity was not one of his strong suits.

Lee had more deals going on at one time than the stock market. I was often furious with him, and I would push him around. The only thing I ever did that really affected him was to tell him that he was not capable of loving anyone with a real love. I had seen him use and abuse so many members of the opposite sex. I think that revelation scared him.

We had just recently moved from Bacon Street where I had been living alone in a one-room studio apartment with my dog Coke. I ended up taking in Lee, as well as about four other people. The only privacy was the bathroom, if you were lucky enough to get in there.

One such person I had taken in was an independent roofer named Rico Valdez. My first meeting with him was at Lee's request to try to get Rico to pay the money he owed Lee for a roofing job he had helped him with. When Rico came to the door, I had a strong suspicion that he would be more to tangle with than I than I really wanted to on that particular morning. Rico was half black and half Mexican, and when he came to the door, his bronzed chest looked like something out of a weightlifters magazine. I politely asked him to cough up the money he owed Lee, (partly because Lee owed me rent money), and he said he would the next week. I said "Great!" He didn't pay Lee the next week, but the answer was good enough for me at that particular time.

Rico lived with his girlfriend and their two kids. A couple of weeks after our first meeting, Rico came to my door in a panic. "The man's after me! Can you put me up for awhile?" I obliged. Rico seemed very grateful. He acted awfully weird when he did drugs, particularly when he did methamphetamines. He would go into a paranoid state. Everyone was a cop, and everyone was out to get him! He loved to read outlaw cowboy books where the outlaw was the hero. I had a strong suspicion that he often assumed the role of these black-hatted heroes and then took great pleasure in pretending the "law" was after him. It was a very updated version of cowboys and Indians. One night after Lee, Rico, and a diminutive man accurately nicknamed Shorty were partying, Rico went berserk. He beat up his two "friends", accusing them of ripping him off and of being "pigs". I really didn't like Lee too much, so I wasn't overly concerned.

A few days later, Rico and I were at Mack's house. We took some blotter acid, and walked up to the Jack-In-The-Box about a quarter of a mile away. A guy would deal barbiturates out of his bedroom window that faced the alley next to the restaurant. I thought we could pick up a couple of downers for later so as to not stay up all night on the acid. The next stop would have been for a burger and fries. I used to bum French fries late at night from the Jack-In-The-Box, if I was out of cash.

I tapped the window of my friend's bedroom. "Do you have any downs?" My friend, whom I never saw face to face because of the dimly lit bedroom, came to the window, opened it up partially, and said "Sure, Clifton." I handed him a couple of bucks, and he handed me the downers. I gave Rico a couple, and out of the blue he started yelling at me, "You ripped me off!" I thought this was strange because I was the one who turned Rico on to the the acid and the downers. My friend told me to split, and shut the window. Rico began calling me a narc, and ranting about who knows what. It dawned on me that Rico was coming on to the acid and couldn't handle it. He was flipping out!

"I'm not a narc, I'm your friend! What are you talking about?" I pleaded.

"You're going to die!" Rico proclaimed.

He started punching me. It was a warm summer night, and all I had on was a pair of Levis and no shirt or shoes. We ended up rolling in the alley and crunching the broken glass as we punched it out. We fought all the way back to the Del Wood Apartments where I lived. Rico wore me out. I ended up lying on the front lawn of the apartment. I saw neighbors peering through the curtains as Rico pulled his belt off and began whipping my back with the buckle side. Out of the corner of my eye I saw a police car slowly cruising up Bacon St. It kept going. At that time O.B. was a dangerous place, even for cops. The unwritten policy was "look the other way" if you are patrolling alone and are out-gunned. I lay there limp and beaten. Rico Valdez finally took off, probably feeling like the outlaw that rode off into the sunset after chalking up another victim. One side of my face was destroyed and I felt like I'd been run over by a train hauling Mac trucks. I made it upstairs and collapsed.

The week before, I had to throw someone off these

same stairs, because Lee had ripped off the guy's hair dryer while he was staying with us. Now the guy wildly swung a golf club at my head. I ducked, but he put a hole in my door. I then proceeded to throw him off of the second story. He didn't fall far and was not injured. I hadn't stolen his hair dryer. It was that type of thing that made me constantly upset with Lee.

When I managed to stagger inside after the fight with Rico, no one else was home. I was glad because I needed my bed and privacy. My girlfriend came over the next day. I only peered out with the "good" side of my face showing. After she asked to come in, I had to explain to her what happened. She took care of me that day.

Soon after this I bought another gun. My .22 had been ripped off at the Allied Gardens house during a rumble. I didn't see Rico Valdez until one night the neighbors yelled up to Lee and me, "Valdez is back!" Our whole courtyard came out of their apartments as I grabbed my bat and ran down the stairs. I didn't bring the gun. I saw Valdez and he had a smile on his face as he taunted Lee and me. I held the wooden bat back as Valdez approached. I knew what he was trying to do. I believe he thought I didn't have it in me to swing the bat at his head, so he could grab it, and beat my brains in. There was a fraction of a second where it could have gone either way. I could have taken his head off, but I chose not to. I ran up the street and called the police from a pay phone. Local calls were a dime. Lee ran also, but to where I wasn't sure.

Part of me wanted to kill Rico Valdez, but I couldn't bring myself to it. I left the gun upstairs. Perhaps I believed that there was a chance Valdez could be salvaged. I'm not sure. Rico was arrested for aggravated assault and did some time because it was not his first offense.

I saw Rico years later when I had been clean and sober for awhile. He seemed almost normal. When I asked him how his family was, he said the kids weren't really his. He said he had some tests done, and the blood type was different. It seemed funny that they looked just like him, though. He was no longer living with his girlfriend. I am convinced this man was still living a life of self-delusion. Given the right circumstances, he could go off again.

But the violence in Ocean Beach didn't hold a candle to what was brewing in San Carlos. At the same time Rico Valdez and I were punching it out, a sixteen-year-old girl in San Carlos had delusions of her own.

CHAPTER 7

I HATE MONDAYS; THE BRENDA SPENCER STORY

"On Monday morning you gave me no warning of what was to be. / On Monday evening I thought you'd still be here with me." The Mamas and Papas

It was early Monday morning, and I was waiting for my assignment as a substitute custodian via telephone from the San Diego Unified School District Custodial Office. I got my assignment and called my parents who still lived out in San Carlos to see how they were doing. My mom answered the phone but I could hardly hear her for all the noise in the background. It was police helicopters. My mom told me there was a shooting going on at my old school; Cleveland Elementary. I turned on the news, and all channels were covering it. A sixteen-year-old high school student named Brenda Spencer was shooting from her front window at the little kids coming to school.

She injured some of the small children seriously, and in the process, killed the principal and the building services supervisor as they were trying to protect the students. The SWAT team finally captured Brenda, and her only answer for the tragedy was "I don't like Mondays, this livens up the day." Eight children were injured as was police officer Robert Robb. *The San Diego Tribune* called Brenda when the siege was going on and asked her why she was doing this. Her answer was: "I just wanted to. It just popped into my head about last Wednesday, I think." She ended the conversation with "I have to go now. I shot a pig, I think, and I want to shoot some more." Her best friend said Brenda was an avid fan of SWAT type television shows. "When she saw stuff like that, she'd say, 'Oh, wow!'"

In Officer Robb's account of what transpired that day, one gets the feeling of the panic, confusion, and trauma that must have gone through the victims' minds. The following are excerpts from superior court documents:

On or about January 29, 1979, while on duty, Officer Robb responded to an emergency call and reported to Cleveland Elementary School in order to protect the occupants of said school from a rifle attack mounted by defendant Brenda Spencer from within her home at 6356 Lake Atlin Ave. in San Diego, California. Thereafter, Officer Robb arrived at Cleveland Elementary School and undertook to rescue and protect the occupants of said school, including children present on the playground.

At said time defendant Brenda Spencer wrongfully, unlawfully, intentionally, and violently fired rifle shots at Officer Robb thereby causing a bullet to strike Officer Robb in the neck with said bullet thereafter lodging underneath the shoulder blade of Officer Robb.

On or about December 1978, defendant Wallace E, Spencer purchased a .22 caliber rifle and 600 rounds of ammunition for said rifle and gave said rifle and ammunition to defendant Brenda Spencer.

The actions of defendant Wallace E. Spencer as set forth in paragraph III above were negligent in that at all times herein mentioned defendant Wallace E. Spencer was aware that defendant Brenda Spencer had a history of anti-social behavior, a dangerous propensity towards violence, had in fact committed violence, and had a history of drug use and emotional problems.

At the time defendant Wallace E. Spencer gave defendant Brenda Spencer the aforesaid rifle and ammunition, defendant Wallace E. Spencer did such act recklessly and in reckless and wanton disregard of the possible consequences to the public, including law enforcement officers, because he knew or should have known that said conduct would unreasonably expose the public, including Officer Robb, to probable serious harm for reasons set forth in paragraph IV above.

Here's an excerpt from the deposition of Officer Robb:

Q. At this juncture where you were at the corner of the building, and you yelled out to this woman, did it look like she was taking cover or something?

A. No. She looked like she was in hysterics.

Q. Is there a reason why you yelled out to her rather

77

than just going over to her?

A. Yes.

Q. What was that?

A. Because there was about, I'd say, sixty feet of open space between me and her.

Q. And what was the reason that you didn't just simply run over that sixty feet of open space to talk to her?

A. 'Cause I didn't know where the shots were coming from at that time.

Q. At that time you were apprehensive of the fact that someone might be shooting, and that you might get shot?

A. Yes.

Q. So at that point again when you yelled to this woman you were aware that there was a hazard of being shot in the area, correct?

A. I was aware that there was that possibility.

Q. Where were you when you first were aware of the possibility that there was a hazard that you would get shot?

A. That's hard to say. I imagine that I was aware of the fact that I could possibly get shot from the time I got the radio call.

Q. Now at that time you were at the Cleveland Elementary School, you were on duty as a police officer, correct?

A. Yes.

Q. After you shouted at this woman across this open

space of approximately 60 feet, did you then start to run towards the steps that you were going down?

A. I ran down the hallway to where the steps were at, yes.

Q. When you got to the steps, did you then run down the steps?

A. Not immediately, no.

Q. How long did you wait there?

A. A matter of seconds. I'm not sure how many.

Q. And then after waiting near the steps for this very short period of time, you then started running down the steps?

A. Yes.

Q. And as you were running down the steps is the first time you heard gunfire while you were at the Cleveland Elementary school; is that correct?

A. As I remember, yes.

Q. And it was the purpose in running down the steps to avoid being struck by any shooting?

A. Yes. That's why I was running.

Q. And when you heard the shots, I believe you indicated that you dove into the bushes or the brush?

A. Yes.

Q. And was the purpose of your diving in there again to prevent being struck by this hazard of someone shooting at you?

A. Yes.

Q. And was that also the reason that you were in prone position when you were trying to get your trauma kit out, and to assist these two people that were wounded near you?

A. Yes.

Q. And so then you were reaching for your trauma kit is the next thing that happened?

A. Right.

Q. And what happened after that?

A. Well, I opened it up, took out some dressings, and rolled over to Mr. Suchar, the custodian, to where he was lying.

Q. And what happened?

A. And I started checking him for gunshot wounds. I found a wound on the front side of his chest and another one on the back side. I applied a dressing onto both of them and then I rolled from where he was at, and started checking the other wounded people to put dressings on them also.

Q. Were you in prone position at that time; do you remember?

A. No. I was lying down, rolling over.

Q. After you got back to Mr. Wragg, did you apply some dressings to his wounds?

A. No. I didn't get a chance to.

Q. What happened?

A. Well, as I went back to him, and unbuttoned his

shirt, and I saw the wound on the front of him, and I kind of pulled myself over the top of him, and was reaching over him, and lifted him up to check his back side. And at that point that is when I got shot.

Q. Did you know at the time that you had been shot?

A. Well, I didn't know that I was actually shot, but I knew something had happened. I knew that I had been shot at, and I felt it had hit my back. But I thought it had bounced off my bulletproof vest.

Q. Did you say anything to anybody at that time?

A. Not at that particular instance, no. I just laid him back down, and then I rolled back over to where my kit was laying, because the kit was laying between the two of them. And when I when I got back over to where my kit was, Officer—I think it was Officer Amos asking me if I had been hit. And I believe that I replied that I didn't know or I wasn't sure, something to that effect.

Q. At the point in time where you felt something hit you, do you remember hearing gunfire at that time?

A. Yeah. I heard gunfire at the time that I felt being hit.

Q. How many shots did you hear at that time, if you can remember?

A. I'm not sure.

Q. What did you feel that made you think that you had been shot?

A. Well, the only thing that I felt was I felt something hit back there.

Q. You are reaching behind your neck?

A. Yeah, back there.

Q. Behind your right shoulder?

A. Yes.

There is more, but the account by one brave officer demonstrates the senselessness and utter madness that went down on January 29, 1979. Interestingly, Daniel T. Broderick III, the attorney representing four of the students that were shot, also died violently. He and his new wife Linda were shot to death by his jealous and driven ex-wife, Betty Broderick.

Brenda was given the rifle as a Christmas present from her dad. Also, her friends said she had built a fort in the garage and dug a tunnel in the backyard. Today there is a memorial to the principal, Burton Wragg, and the building services supervisor, Michael Suchar, at the Education Center and the Cleveland site.

As a child, I looked at Cleveland Elementary as a safe haven from a difficult family situation. There was security and friendship there. It has been hard to imagine having the wonderful cloud of childhood fantasy instantly burned to ashes by the intrusion of a dangerously paranoid world. It was the same spot where I held hands with a girl for the first time, hopped on a bus for winter camp in the sixth grade, and left with my diploma never to return. Life had been mercilessly rubbed out. San Carlos was no longer the

Ozzie and Harriet wonderland. It had become a "Nightmare on Elm Street."

Brenda had been living in a split-up family situation. Her father, Wally, was working at San Diego State University at that time, and her mother lived elsewhere. One can only speculate how torn-up this young girl was on the the inside to act as she did. Prison shrinks are probably still working on it.

Could the Altstadt murders a few years prior and a couple of blocks away have planted seeds in Brenda's mind? Did the same diabolical cloud transform this young woman into a monster with a seared conscience? Will she ever come to grips with the reality of her crimes? Maybe some day we will know.

CHAPTER 8

THE SUICIDE SOLUTION

"I think I'm gonna kill myself, commit a little suicide."
Elton John

Greg Lloyd was always a very strange kid. A nerd before the term gained popularity. He was a tall, gangly, bespectacled young man who wore a strap to hold his glasses on. In junior high he was always getting punched, kicked, and generally beaten on. He was extremely skinny, and his pants were always too high for him. His white socks showed in their entirety. When Greg walked forward, it looked as though he had to keep moving in order to not fall on his face because of the momentum. I guess I would have walked quickly in order to not get beat up all the time. In junior high I did not talk with him much, because I didn't want my reputation stained. For a time in high school I actually got friendly with Greg, mainly because for a short season I actually grew up and realized the value of a human, even though I would repress what I knew was right to try to find my identity in years to come. It reminds me of that Dylan song, "My Back Pages," and the one verse that sticks out: "Ah, but I was so much older then, I'm younger than that now." Only in my case, it was a relapse into a frightening concept of life. I didn't think I would reach thirty, and nearly didn't.

Greg had a crush on a girl named Carol. She had always been quiet and unassuming. Her complexion was white, and her features made her look like the tin man in the "Wizard of Oz" but with blond hair. She was always very nice, and had her small group of girlfriends. It seemed like Greg all of the sudden matured, and stopped being that goofy kid. He dressed better, and even at such a large high school like Patrick Henry, didn't seemed to get hassled by the guys who used to give him a hard time. This school was like a major city where you didn't have to cross someone's path unless you wanted to. It seemed like things were going fine with this pair. They were always together.

Greg's dad owned and operated a gas station off of Navajo Road, and Greg was working there after school and on the weekends. His responsibility impressed me. He wasn't the type who would go to college but would continue in the work force and probably do fine.

It was soon after graduation in 1973 and I saw the news. Greg had committed suicide by shooting himself in the head. I had heard that he had been shunned by Carol soon before this. Perhaps Greg's identity had been so wrapped up in Carol's that without her life wasn't worth living. If someone could have convinced him that he would get over it (Carol), and in no time someone else would come along. I know the hurt of getting dropped. It happened to me right around the same time. It took a while to heal. Maybe Greg exercised the same lack of patience on himself that everyone else had over the years. He felt there was no hope. .

And then there was David Isabell. He lived a couple of blocks south of me, but we didn't have a lot of interaction in grade school, although we were the same age, because he went to Catholic school at this time while I went to Cleveland. I thought the uniforms looked so weird. Looking back, this is probably why all the boys who went to Catholic school always picked fights with us "regular" guys. They were on the defensive all the time. I would have been also if I was forced to look like everyone else, (although, one glance at us, and we all looked like clones of one another: madras shirts with madras belts, Converse low top tennis shoes with surfer shirts, then the paisley fad. I was always a year behind the styles and never could afford Converse). Anyway, in my eyes these guys were different.

There was another guy, Phil, from an Italian family who lived close to Dave's house and also went to Catholic school. Phil had one goal in life from the time he was a kid, through high school, when he went to Patrick Henry, and that was to be a boss in the mob. I have never seen anyone so consistent in their childhood fantasies. Phil might be at the bottom of a river right now. I lost track of him.

In junior high, David went to Pershing and we became friends. Upon occasion, we would smoke pot together. I used to have to babysit some kids across the street from my house when I was fifteen, and after I would send them to bed, my buddies would come over and we would toke up.

Dave always seemed to have confidence in himself. He would walk in a bouncing fashion like he had springs built in his shoes, but it looked cool. He had dishwater blond hair, blue eyes, and was somewhat stocky. He, like myself, enjoyed joking around, and didn't seem to take life all that seriously. His older brother Danny was looked up to. He drove a souped-up maroon Falcon that was clean as a whistle. It didn't really seem that Dave tried to live up to Danny's reputation.

When David was just out of high school, he took an interest in a girl that lived across and down the street. Her name was Deanie. She was a year younger than I was, and when we were kids, I hung out some with her little brothers. I always felt this girl would have made a great singer, along the lines of Janis Joplin. You could hear her for miles when she started yelling at someone. She could have been Lucy from the Peanuts strip.

We didn't get along too well in junior high. There was a group of girls that hung out with Deanie. Two of them, Judi and Sheryl, were cousins and lived on our street.

Unfortunately, they and another girl who lived a few blocks away took the same route home from school as I did. They decided I would be the designated hasslee for a time. Adolescence was terrible to Deanie. The zit monster attacked her face like napalm in Laos. In spite of this, I never called her names. Anyway, on the way home from school, they would verbally assault me. I was in eighth grade, and they were in the seventh. I had a pretty good reputation by this time, so I wrongly figured they had some crush on me. Judi was the only one who didn't say anything, (she was also my next door neighbor, and we were always pretty good friends). Her cousin Sheryl was a different story. I really believe she and Deanie took voice lessons together. Sheryl's mouth was the biggest part of her body. Anyway, I just kind of shined them.

This went on for awhile, and I finally got called into my counselor's office, Mr. Henne. Although I was an "A" student, he didn't like me too much. This was the era of the sit-in, and our student body didn't want to be left out. We held a sit-in in front of the school after lunch one day. It was mostly the stoners and rabble rousers. I was right in the middle of it. Anyway, Mr. Henne and I grew apart after this event. I was called into his office because Deanie had accused me of swearing at them on the way home. I couldn't believe it! I tried to tell Mr. Henne I was innocent, but hey, when you have zero credibility, forget it! Guilty until proven innocent. This was the first case of sexual harassment that I was cognizant of. Before Clarence Thomas.

That night Deanie came over and talked to my dad, telling him what had (supposedly) transpired. My dad had always had the ability to read people like a book — this time was no different. He just ignored her. I later filled him in.

As the years went by, Deanie lost the zits and seemed to acquire a more mature attitude in every way. She turned into a very lovely young lady. The suitors began to call. Dave was one of them. I don't know all the details, but rumor has it he fell head over heels in love with her. She didn't feel the same way about him.

Dave blew his own head off before his 21st birthday. Again, someone under the delusion that there is no tomorrow.

I had another friend that lived around the corner from Dave, one block closer to my street. Martin Seifert was a year older than me. He was extremely tall. His freckles made him look like a character out of a Mark Twain book. Martin was a real nice guy, and into his own hobbies. His younger brother Neil was two years younger than me, and a more outgoing person. They had a great family that seemed to care about them.

Well, the drug scene seemed to affect even the nice families. Martin and some guys we grew up with started smoking pot. Some got into dealing drugs, and Neil seemed to get pulled into this aspect of it. LSD was a common pastime of my childhood friends. I was nineteen, and had done acid for years, but it took me back to see these kids who I used to play football in the street frying their brains. Of course, I joined them. It was 1973 and I had just graduated from high school. Neil and his family bought a huge lot on Mt. Helix, which was the wealthy area southeast of San Carlos. I remember splitting a hit of clearlight acid with Martin one summer afternoon. We were trying to clear the driveway at this new house, but I didn't help much. I could hardly do anything for twelve hours but listen to music. Well, the house was finished by October. There was a Halloween party at Martin and Neil's new house. The parents were gone, so we all ate acid. Neil seemed to be the director of events that night. There were so many beautiful girls there, I tried to get to know at least one. I did, but when I found out she was sixteen, I didn't pursue it too much, since I was eighteen and knew about the statutory rape laws.

I thought Neil and Martin had it made in this mansion.

I couldn't have had it more wrong. Neil was a sensitive kid, and LSD was not what he should have been doing. This drug can turn somebody into a paranoid madman, or drive them to schizophrenia. I have seen both. I don't know what happened to Neil, but just a short time after this, he put a plastic bag over his head and purposely suffocated himself. Was it the drugs? I'm positive they had a lot to do with this.

Those people that are out there attempting to advocate the legalization of drugs to curtail the black market will be putting dynamite into the hands of the vulnerable.

Chuck was another kid who was part of the Black Mountain gang. When we were renting a house in Allied Gardens, he would ride his shiny black Shovel Head Harley-Davidson over with his beautiful but wild girlfriend clinging to his back. Kathy had a mind of her own. It seemed like Chuck should have known that she made love to many of his "good Buddies". If he did know, he didn't seem to care. I even tried for Kathy one night, when Chuck was in the living room. She politely said, "Not tonight, Mark". It seems when many drugs are consumed, values go up in smoke with them.

Chuck was a stocky guy with shoulder-length blond hair. He didn't act like the typical biker. He was generally neat and clean and respected his friends.

I can remember partying in our backyard at the house. We had a keg, and anyone was welcome. Anyone but the group that showed up this night.

San Carlos and Allied Gardens probably had a 99% white population. There was an Hispanic family thrown in, and I can remember only four black families. Cleon belonged to one of these. He was "one of the guys" and was at the yard kegger when Chuck yelled, "What the f--- was that!"

"It was those f---ing niggers. Let's get 'em!" someone else proclaimed as rocks landed around us.

Someone took Rick to the hospital as the rest of us jumped in our cars to look for these blacks who had thrown rocks over our house when we kicked them out of our party. There was a mass exodus.

Cleon didn't join us.

At this time in the early Seventies, suburban whites did not care for any minorities and were very suspicious of them. But I know the same things would have happened if white kids would have tried to party with blacks in their neighborhood. Segregation had been outlawed just ten years prior to this.

Someone grabbed my .22 semi-automatic rifle while Chuck, Tony, and I piled into a truck and sped off.

No one ever found those guys. Rick had some long-term partial paralysis in his right arm, and some dizzy spells. My .22 never found its way home.

Chuck was forever a part of San Carlos. He would fight for his friends to the death but sometimes seemed to have his priorities screwed up.

One time Chuck and Tony were working at a construction site and Tony got stung by a bee. He is allergic to the venom, and didn't have his adrenaline kit with him. Tony was trying to express the need to get to the hospital because otherwise he would die. Chuck was driving his truck, and had at least a half-tank of gas.

Somehow Chuck was missing the concept. He pulled into a gas station, filled the tank, and was going to check the tires until Tony, in his increasingly weak voice pleaded with him:

"What the hell are you doing?! I'm going to die you dumb f---!"

"Oh, okay," Chuck said in his mild mannered way. They hopped into the truck and made it to the hospital.

Chuck always had a dream of being a roady for the big-name rock bands. The dream finally started happening for him. He and his girl Kathy broke it off, and Chuck seemed to enjoy his time on the road.

A big name promoter promised Chuck work with some of the bigger rock groups. The promoter went back on his word, and one day this tough, quiet, nice guy had had enough. Instead of taking it out on the promoter, Chuck went home and blew his own brains out. This was in the mid 1980's. I hadn't seen him in over a decade when I heard the news.

Earlier I wrote about my friend Jon Jackson. The kid who lit the mail box on fire with David Allen Lucas and later became my roommate when we were both eighteen. Shortly after Jon, Randy, and I moved out from the townhouse we were renting in La Mesa, (it's a wonder anyone would rent to three rowdy teenagers), Jon got married to this girl who was a few years older than he. She had already been through one divorce. Jon was always a solid guy. No one knew what triggered him to blow his brains out after his marriage broke up. I always felt Jon would bounce back from anything. I was wrong.

Is this purely coincidence that five people, some who knew each other well, some who just knew the face and name, but all lived so close to each other, would kill themselves? I believe this phenomenon defies national averages. The black cloud of despair, hopelessness, and suicide seemed to grow, flourish, and darken the hearts of these former friends of mine. I wish I would have known how desperate they were. I hope we as a society are heeding and taking seriously the tell-tale signs in our family, with friends and neighbors in regard to this drastic choice.

CHAPTER 9

THE KIDS ARE ALRIGHT

"Take a long holiday, let your children play." The Doors

A Star is Born — The Real Annette Bening Story:

I suppose for every story with a sad ending, there is one of success. The same holds true for San Carlos. Some people did manage to break out of the constraints of peer pressure, or whatever pressure was inflicting these tragic results on our community. One particular family stands out.

I have already mentioned Brad Bening. Who would have thought Brad's little sister Annette would be the superstar she is today? Actually, of all the Bening kids, Brad was the most likely to be the thespian in the family. In ninth grade, Brad did an Elvis impression of "Ain't Nothing But A Hound Dog" for a play, and immediately became famous. He was a true character.

In junior high we became friends. It seemed anyone was welcomed into the Bening home. Brad lived above San Carlos in Del Cerro with his parents, older sister Jane (who was my sister's age), younger brother Byron, and little sister Annette. It seemed that their parents had a deep trust in their four children, and that they realized that certain phases would be temporary — even the drug counter-culture. Brad was an average student with a wild imagination. Jane excelled in school. Annette was wild but committed to drama and acting at a young age. Byron was also an average student. The unconditional love that their parents exhibited seemed to carry the kids through the self-destructive adolescence. Jane became a medical doctor, Brad became a lawyer, and Annette became a well-known actress with many movies such as *The Grifters, Bugsy,* and *Regarding Henry.*

I can remember partying with Brad and the guys, knowing that if I went home, my parents would have found out I was smoking dope and drinking. Brad's house was kind of a refuge for his buddies. I spent many Friday nights on Brad's couch. One thing I can remember from Mr. and Mrs. Bening was very little condemnation and a very wide welcome mat. I know they were not oblivious to what was going on, but rather had a hope for their children that reflected also in their attitude to their children's friends. Maybe they possessed the secret ingredients that were missing in some of the other families — faith, hope and love.

Annette began dating a good friend of mine, Marty, when she was just out of high school in 1976. I was living in Ocean Beach with her best friend's fiancé, and she met Marty at our house. In spite of our lousy influence on her, Annette had a driving force that allowed her to rise above even her affections for Marty. I can remember when Annette was over at our house before she and Marty were dating. She was standing outside talking to a guy who seemed to be pressing her for some kind of commitment. Annette had the whole situation under control. The truth was she was dumping this guy. He seemed like the drama class type, and Annette was more woman than this guy could handle.

Marty and Annette had a good summer together, and we did our share of partying. Marty was becoming attached, and it seemed to me that Annette knew that this also was going to be a temporary situation. At the end of summer, Annette ended the relationship with Marty. She soon moved to New York and began a long, grueling road to success in acting. One of my best friends, Tony, married Sue, (Annette's best friend at the time), in September of 1976. It was a spectacular ceremony. Brad Bening was Tony's best man, and "Hank" the Mongol and I were groomsmen. Annette was the maid of honor, and Sue's sister Karen was a bridesmaid. It took place in the large Methodist church in Mission Valley. It was the first time I ever wore a tux. The reception was at Sue's house which was next door to Benings. From what I remember, my girlfriend got extremely upset with me for leaving with another girl.

I'm positive that a loving, nurturing home life has a lot to do with the way kids turn out. Even the strong winds of peer pressure can't keep the youth down who has goals in life. Goals are not all there is to fulfilling the future, but having a goal is better than the alternative. The Benings were by no means the perfect family, and the Bening kids did not become perfect adults, but having the knowledge that their parents were behind them endowed them with the confidence to rise to their potential.

Another one of my best friends, Shaun, not only survived in life, but excelled. It would have been hard for anyone to see it when we were younger. His life has been an influence on mine, as I have put forth in this book.

I met Shaun back in 1967 in seventh grade. He was the only kid I knew who had parents who not only allowed him to have long hair, but who would challenge any school administrator that would say any different. Shaun's dad was a probation officer and seemed to have an understanding relationship with his four daughters and two sons. Shaun's mom was always very nice, but concerned about what was happening. Shaun's room was HIS!--his parents respected his privacy enough to let Shaun have his own place. They knew Shaun did drugs. I believe they had the foresight to know that he would be an adult who would be accountable for his actions, and gave him some room to grow. Invading his privacy would have cut off any trust that they would have had. I can see where small things like this helped mold Shaun into person who thought for himself, learned from his mistakes, and had trust as a foundation for all his relationships. Apparently drugs were a passing symptom for those who had goals and aspirations.

But back in those days, drugs were a lifestyle, an idol. Shaun, Kirk, and I went to a Led Zeppelin concert at the Sports Arena in 1970. LSD was so readily available, you could pick your color, strength, and so forth. The police did not know how to deal with the dilemma yet. Out in the parking lot, sales were going on every second. This particular night we ate some brown barrel acid, and some mescaline. By the time the concert was over, I was seeing words coming out of people's mouths. We were so stoned, we would spend the night in Shaun's backyard in a tent. Shaun's dad gave us a ride home, and had to listen to us laugh all night long in the backyard. We were all fifteen years old. For years Shaun and I lived together, dealt drugs together, fought together, got arrested together, and grew together,

In 1974 I was living in Lakeside. Shaun and I were drunk, so I let him crash on my couch. After a couple of hours he woke me up. He had forgotten his grandma was coming to town, so when he remembered, he wanted to get home and sober up for her. I protested about driving him, (Shaun had lost his license for two previous episodes when we were in his Corvair Manza. Both times we were so blitzed I'm surprised we lived.) I was on probation for three years for my first drunk driving conviction. I had to go to class as part of the sentence.

After much protesting, I conceded to take Shaun home. I was extremely ticked-off at Shaun, so I floored my Nova up Pepper Drive in Lakeside. I ran a stop sign, and ended up running into a barricade at the intersection. We promptly got out and pulled the bumper off of the front wheels.

We were drunk, and both of us had taken whites, (a type of prescription speed), earlier in the evening. We had been at Sonny's brother-in-law's house trying out as singers in his band. We discovered that we couldn't sing while we were all partying and drinking from a keg. Someone had the whites, so we all had some. Now my blood-alcohol content was surely high, but because of the speed, I was awake in a strange way. The sheriffs found us trying to get my car going and promptly took us to jail. Our first stop was the Sheriff's substation in Santee. I knew it was all over for my license, so Shaun and I just proceeded to make light of the situation. We both had extremely long hair, and must have been quite an amusement for the police since they were laughing harder than Shaun and I were. We both ended up in jail. I did lose my license and had to take anti-buse every other day at the probation department. Anti-buse is a drug that will react violently to alcohol. It can kill you if you drink with it. A few months into the program, I didn't go in for my anti-buse because I had a warrant for my arrest. The minute I would have shown up, I would have been cuffed.

After three days without anti-buse, I drank one six-pack of beer, and my stomach seemed to be fine. I drank my second six-pack, this time talls. I drank Coors because I didn't want to test the anti-buse too much. That didn't help. Whatever residue of anti-buse was in my system kicked in. I lay in my bathroom in Santee puking my guts out. I really thought I was going to die. I still didn't believe what my probation officer said about me self-destructing.

When I finally turned myself in and went to court, I resumed my anti-buse, or so they thought. It's hard to keep an alcoholic from drinking. I noticed that the anti-buse looked a lot like a B-complex vitamin I took. I decided to take the B-complex to the probation department with me. When I grabbed my designated bottle of anti-buse and opened the lid, I secretly had two B-complexes in my hand. I faked pouring the anti-buse in my hand, and showed the probation officer the B-complex as I put it into my mouth. I just wonder how they never noticed that the bottle never emptied!

Shaun and I had many more bizarre and strange tales, but the bottom line is — by the grace of God we got out alive.

Shaun always had a strong Irish work ethic. I can remember him choosing to cut his hair so he could work at the El Cajon Speedway. He said, "I guess I can't hang around the heads for awhile, but I've go to make some bucks." His head was always on straight, even when in the clouds. Drugs did take away a great part of the maturing process. I have a theory about many of the drugs that were doing. The psychedelic and hallucinogenic drugs were either weeds or fungus such as various mushrooms that possessed powerful ingredients, or cactus like peyote that made you sick before you would come on to its power. If you didn't throw up, you would be sick to your stomach for hours. Even LSD is made from the mold off of rye bread. All of these drugs were created from something dead, dying, and obviously not put here for human consumption, and their effects are hallucinations — things that are not. Not Carlos Castaneda's "separate reality," but a false one.

Since the writing of the first edition of this book, I have changed my position on marijuana. I do believe there is medicinal components of cannabis, valuable for cancer patience going through chemotherapy and for relief from many other illnesses.

It is interesting that people who get involved hallucenigenic drugs often get interested in the occult and the like. It is also interesting that according to Biblical history, there was no death, no weeds, no fungus, and no mold, until the fall of man when Satan began controlling the world's activities. These drugs hold little benefit for man, but were sent to distort reality by the one who was the first to lie. I'm convinced drugs played a major role in the demise of our "lost generation." Nevertheless, Shaun, as well as a multitude of others in San Carlos, came away from these crazy years unscathed. They rose above the storms of destruction and were set free from the bondage of peer pressure to make a life for themselves.

CHAPTER 10

FROM SATANIC SACRIFICES TO FAMILY BARBEQUES

"Cha, cha, cha changes..." David Bowie

The "Heart Transplant" of Kirk Dubois:

In 1971 part of our gang became plugged into what was called the "Jesus Movement." Things were looking shaky for our idols: Jim Morrison of the Doors, Jimi Hendrix, and Janis Joplin all died within months of each other. The first time I saw Jimi Hendrix I had just turned fourteen. He came to the Sports Arena and the tickets were only $2.75 each. The second time I saw him was in 1970, also at the Sports Arena. I don't remember much about the concert except breaking open Seconals, and digesting the putrid white powder straight. I also saw the Doors that summer, and remember Jim Morrison lying on the stage on his back smoking a joint. It was a boring concert.

Our local heroes were dropping like flies also. I can still

remember hitchhiking to a friend's house with Shaun and Kirk to pick up some pot. It was the summer of 1970. Two of the local "heads" that hung around San Carlos Recreation Center picked us up. We were stoked because we knew we could cop some drugs from these two guys. Roger Grove and Paul Powell had us climb in the back of Roger's old Thunderbird.

"What's happening, dudes?" Paul asked in a very mellowed way.

"Nothing, man," said Kirk, our spokesman. "We're just trying to cop some pot. Do you guys have any?" Pretty bold for a fifteen-year-old to say to the old dudes. (Old meaning 19!")

"No, man. We've got something much better," Paul bragged as he pulled out a baggie of small, round, red tablets. I knew what reds were, and these were shaped differently. But they looked inviting, whatever they were.

"These are a more powerful red", Paul said. "Take them with hot water, and you'll come on faster." Such wisdom from these long-haired sages of hippie-dom. Roger was driving towards University Avenue, where we were headed, but was weaving more and more as we progressed. I was looking forward to these drugs. Ditching reality was becoming my favorite pastime.

We bought a bunch, and still kept enough money for a half-lid of pot, about a half-ounce, which cost five dollars. Roger and Paul dropped us off, and we walked the rest of the way to my friend's house to buy pot. We took the Seconals with hot water as the "doctor" ordered. We bought the pot and smoked a couple of joints before leaving.

I could hardly walk. The same with Shaun and Kirk. Somehow we managed to make it home.

In just over a month after this, in the early fall of 1970, Roger Grove and Paul Powell both overdosed and died within one week from each other from ingesting too many Seconals. My friend John, who had sold us the pot, broke up with his girlfriend, and ended up going off of the deep end, robbing a house and having a shoot-out with the cops. He was wounded and, because he was a juvenile, did some time in the California Youth Authority.

Things were beginning to unravel.

What was perplexing was the sense of doom that many of us felt. Kirk had a library of books dealing with witchcraft and psychic phenomena. He wouldn't let anyone touch the books.

The word occult literally means "hidden in darkness." Kirk, at one point, began a three-part ritual that would commit his life to the dark side. He only got through the first two nights! Something stopped him. He challenged God and said, "If you're really out there, prove it!

That weekend in 1971, Kirk, Bill the "Animal," and a Volkswagen full of other stoners left for Laguna Beach to pick up some LSD. This is where the Brotherhood of

Eternal Love was making and selling some of the strongest acid ever made — *orange sunshine.* Taco Bell was where all the hippies used to congregate — hundreds and hundreds at once, uninterrupted by police — to buy and sell drugs. While the guys were finding the acid, a Hispanic young man in a suit and tie parted the crowd. Mind you, everyone else had on Levi jeans and hair down to their rear ends. He came up to Kirk and asked him if he wanted to know Jesus. Kirk was stunned and very much afraid to say no because this was definitely an answer to his challenge, and afraid to say yes because of the guys. The man grabbed Kirk's hands and prayed some prayer over him. That night everyone ate some acid. The tablets were four-man hits, which meant four people could get stoned out of their minds on one hit. Kirk had consumed two four-man hits! Eight people could have been tripping all night on this dosage.

The driver got as far as Torrey Pines State Beach and had to pull over because he and everyone else was beginning to peak. That is, everyone but Kirk. He didn't even get high. There seemed to be a separate reality working on him.

Within a few weeks Kirk and a bunch of the gang found this group of former outlaw bikers who had been in jail, on drugs, etc. and had become born-again Christians. They were renting a small house on El Cajon Blvd., and had Bible studies on Tuesdays and Thursdays. The average age of the Bible study flock was seventeen. The house would fill up to overflowing with converted hippies. The Animal, his brother, me, and a bunch of our mutual friends had started to show up there. But Kirk was the only one who lasted. Over the years, many of us who had seen the reality of this change never forgot it and gravitated back to it later in life.

Later that year, the Animal overdosed on Seconals at school. He had made a rapid retreat, as we all did, (except Kirk), back to the old way of doing things. Still, I'm sure Bill never forgot the goodness he also tasted at this time.

That summer, 1971, while I was hanging around at the El Cajon Boulevard house, before I took a plunge back into drugs, I got plugged into a group founded by Leonard Hart. The name may not be familiar to you, but his son is Mickey Hart, drummer for the Grateful Dead. Leonard started the Inter-Faith Center. I always wondered why he wanted the media around while we had public baptisms at La Jolla Cove. Come to find out Leonard ripped-off the Dead while he was their manager and used the money to start this ministry. That bummed me out, but I knew it wasn't God's fault. Leonard and I didn't talk much after we learned about the theft. Leonard died in prison.

Speaking of the Grateful Dead, have you ever wondered who was responsible for the art work that graced their album covers? If you haven't seen this work, the skeletal figures are drawn in various animated positions that can usually be seen playing music. One artist for the Grateful Dead was named Phil Garris. He was a Mission Beach local in the Seventies.

When I was living in Santee with the Animal and company, I felt it was time to get my act together, so I signed up at Grossmont College again to take two classes. One was guitar.

I was hitchhiking back to our place in Santee and this long-haired guy in a Travel-All picked me up. I had extremely long hair and a beard at this time, so of course there was that camaraderie. I pulled out some Thai weed which we proceeded to smoke, and he asked me if I needed a place to stay. I said YES!

I moved out of the pit and moved into a place with my own bedroom on Halberns Street in Santee. There were three of us: the guy who picked me up, Spur, and Gary. Gary was a large fellow who resembled Santa Claus. Spur was a character. He avoided the draft during that era by driving to the inductee building in Arizona and acting like a complete space cadet. It would have put Arlo Guthrie to shame. Spur went into his burned-out acid freak rendition for me. I wouldn't have drafted him either. My draft number for the Viet Nam war was high, so the war ended in 1975 before mine came up.

Spur worked as a property management handyman. He was a good-looking guy with a slight build. His art work was pretty good. Gary was a heavy-equipment operator. We all were stoners and had a similar philosophy of communal living. We shared most everything — until Donna showed up.

Donna was a blind date for Gary. I honestly think this was Gary's first girlfriend. He was around twenty-five, so it was about time. But I wish he would have waited for someone else. Donna was extremely fat. That didn't bother me so much, but she was also very vindictive and mean. She learned to hate my free spirit quickly. As I said before, we all shared the food. I would catch Donna at midnight porking down on our food, and I would get blamed for it. She ended up moving in. I thought I had landed in hell.

My old girlfriend Debbie was back in my life, which helped matters. When I was living in Lakeside, she had come to visit me after I had run into her at a New Year's Eve party. I had known her since seventh grade, and we had always been good friends. When she came over, the Animal had just moved in a short time before. Well, she ended up making love to the Animal, even though he had a girlfriend. Before she left, she gave me a big kiss and said "Sorry".

Since that time we had re-established our friendship. She and I and some friends all took some LSD and went to Black's Beach, the "swimsuit optional area" of San Diego. I really had a love for Debbie; she was a tall, gorgeous blonde with a great sense of humor. I didn't have the concept of abstinence and did everything a young, heterosexual man would do. I'm afraid our generation, due to its lack of self-control, laid the groundwork for the immorality and rise in sexually transmitted diseases seen ever since. I loved Debbie, and should have treated her the same way I would want my daughters to be treated. Anyway, we had a good relationship. This particular day we became closer than we ever had. Maybe it was the acid, maybe it was just about time.

About this time, Spur met a beautiful red-head named Sue. She was the girlfriend of Phil Garris, the album cover artist. But she was mad at him and moved in with Spur, and Spur asked her to marry him. She said yes, and I thought everything was set. One day she disappeared and left a note describing the feelings for Phil she still had. Spur was bummed out, but pulled out of it. He recovered enough to win Debbie's heart over. To my deep sorrow, she moved in with Spur instead of with me.

I was feeling like a leper in the king's palace — there was Big Donna who hated my guts, my ex-girlfriend making love with my roommate in the next room, and an increased level of hostility between Gary and me. One night when my buddy Shaun was over, Donna came out of her room yelling that we were too loud. I promptly told her where to plant it. Gary came storming out of his room, and we had a physical altercation. He weighed at least 150 pounds more than I did. It was a stalemate. Needless to say, I was told to leave.

I can remember part of a song I wrote and dedicated to Donna while I was learning guitar:

"Hey big mama, take it all back to Texas,

Come on now, if you still can lift it.

Everything comes in "large" there---

They even got extra-large underwear,

So, hey big mama, move it all back to Texas."

It probably will never be a number-one hit on the cowboy countdown, but it did reflect my feelings at the time.

I went to live in Ocean Beach with my old buddy, Tony, his soon-to-be-fiancé's sister, and our dogs. Debbie told me after she and Spur got married that the rose bush outside of Donna and Gary's room wilted and died. The one outside my old room lived and bloomed. This reinforced my feelings about plants being more alive than we think. It doesn't stop me from eating them, though. I just don't eat any I know personally.

All this time Kirk Dubois was doing things that counted for eternity.

Kirk ended up marrying a beautiful girl named Pat, a former Miss La Mesa. They have two daughters and live in Oklahoma. Kirk is the founder and president of Harvest International Ministries-HIM. Kirk's life is without reproach, and the good he is doing for third-world countries is phenomenal.

When I look back, Kirk could have been worse than anyone I have written about. There's something here that involves free-choice, and perhaps some intervention from elsewhere. Years later we found out that a friend of Mr. Dubois had prayed without ceasing for the Dubois family for years. All the members of the Dubois family have become born-again Christians.

CHAPTER 11

THE HEALING OF A FAMILY

"All you need is love, love is all you need." The Beatles

My mother was a very intelligent woman who suffered from manic depression most of her life. It is true that her mood swings, false accusations, and deep depression did affect the family in a way that has taken years to work through. But the last couple of years she quit Valiums and really tried to be a good wife and mother. She even learned how to actually enjoy watching football on TV. This was a miracle to my dad, who was a die-hard Charger fan.

In 1981, my mother came down with cancer of the lymph nodes. After all those years of declaring how much she wanted to die and actually attempting suicide a number of times through overdosing on drugs, the reality of impending death hit her hard. When my sister and I were just kids, my mother would pull us aside from time to time and whisper "secrets" to us. One time she had told me she only had a few months to live because she had cancer. She made me promise not to tell anyone. She had made this up just to get sympathy, but I didn't know it at the time. Well, now her wish came true. I remember being alone with her in the dining room of their home on a visit shortly after the doctor gave the diagnosis. She cried out to me, "I don't want to die!" This seemed like the first time that she ever valued her existence on this earth. My father stayed by her side day and night as the cancer grew worse and the radiation proved futile. But there was an interesting dichotomy occurring here. My mother made peace with the Creator of the Universe, and although her body was deteriorating daily, her spiritual growth flourished hourly. She had a peace that she had never in her life possessed. The last nine months of my mother's life was the best that she and I shared together.

I forgave her for the torture she inflicted on me — no matter whether she meant to. So many nights I had lain awake wondering why she hated my guts, as she lay in her bed in a drugged or drunken stupor, declaring her disdain for her family. She also forgave me for the years of rebellion that caused me to leave home at seventeen and actually tell her that I hated her. We learned that love does heal a multitude of deep scars. This whole scenario reminded me of a verse, "Unless a seed falls into the ground and dies, it will not bear any fruit."

The cancer took my mother's life in August of 1982, three weeks after her sixty-first birthday, but I know she departed this life with the peace that her family loved her. I am not saying that cancer was the best thing that ever happened to her, but the shock that the revelation of her mortality delivered to her made her value the most important things in life. My sister gave her a grandson just months before she died. Her life was not in vain.

I went through quite a bit in 1979. I was recovering from hepatitis (the more curable form than the kind I would later have to fight), got a new job as a permanent custodian, and moved away from everyone — from my buddies in San Carlos to my "business associates" in Ocean Beach.

I rented a house in Pacific Beach that seemed rather out of place. There were large houses surrounding my small cottage, but the yard was huge, perfect for my dog. I was renting from the Piatkowski's, a Polish family who had escaped their homeland. They gave me a great break on rent. It was in this small, quiet home where I came to grips with my life. I needed to get away from the influences that were bringing me down.

My friend Kirk called me from time to time and asked if I was thinking about Jesus at all. And the fact of the matter was that I was thirsty for the peace and comfort of knowing that my life was headed in the right direction. After talking to Kirk, my mind was flooded with thoughts of all the people I had hurt directly or indirectly. No man is an island — his everyday life affects everyone in his path. People who justify destroying their own lives by saying that they aren't hurting anyone else are fooling themselves. Then the thought hit me. It was a truth that I had hidden deep down in my soul. *I could be forgiven!* There was no way I could "make everything right" that I had done wrong. But I envisioned a large chalkboard wiped clean. The only person who could wipe it clean was the Person who earned the right by standing in for me. Jesus Christ!

That very night I was watching *Saturday Night Live!* on television. I was looking forward to seeing Bob Dylan as the musical guest. To my surprise, he was singing songs about getting your life right. One of the songs was *"You Got To Serve Somebody."* This song affirmed that there was no middle of the road — either you serve God or the devil. I remember thinking that the person I had looked up to all these years as a spokesman for the philosophy of the young was singing a new tune — one that I had long been trying to shut out. The song assured me I was accountable for my actions. I had no one else to blame but myself for the poor choices I had made over the years. The other song he sang was *"When You Gonna Wake Up?"* I truly needed to wake up. These songs were just for me.

The next day I flushed my cocaine and high-grade Columbian pot down the toilet. I got on my knees in my living room and asked God to forgive me and to take the rest of my life. I was suffering from extreme guilt. Many shrinks say guilt is bad, but I don't think so. I think it needs to be dealt with properly. I could now see the shallowness, emptiness, and fruitlessness of the last ten or so years of my life. I could have easily become a statistic a number of times. I alone am accountable for me. I alone make the the decisions that affect my future. I hold no animosity or hatred for anyone in my past. I have learned to put it all behind me, and move forward as a new man. The guilt is gone.

CHAPTER 12

POST-STORM ASSESSMENT

"I can see clearly now-the rain is gone." Johnny Nash

With modern technology, it is easy to see climatic changes via satellite and other weather equipment. Now the only people who stick around for a hurricane are the thrill-seekers who suffer from a false sense of immortality, or people like the old man who thought he would brave out Mt. St. Helens when it erupted with a fierceness that made a slightly smaller version of the Grand Canyon in its path.

But who could see the raging storm that tore the squeaky-clean community of San Carlos apart? It was a slow-building storm that fed on itself as it grew. The more it consumed in its path, the hungrier it got.

For some, the nightmare goes on. The Animal is again in trouble with the law while out on parole.

In August of 2009, Munz pled guilty to Count One of the indictment in *United States vs. Ruben Cavazos*. It all had to do with the war between the Mongols and the Hell's Angels. He was to sentenced to between 70 to 97 months. The war between the Mongols and the Angels goes on still, as does Mike's personal war.

David Allen Lucas is still proclaiming his innocence as

he awaits the gas chamber on death row at San Quentin. I was at a San Carlos reunion recently, and I talked with an old schoolmate who was David's best friend growing up. He was a level headed kid, and I always wondered how two friends who seemed so opposite, could be so close. David was his best man at his wedding. He received letters from Lucas, and is convinced that he is innocent. He admits that Lucas had a crazy streak in him, but felt there was no way he could be a rapist/murderer. At this time Lucas' lawyer is Alex Landon who was accused of aiding the 1972 inmate escape from Chino in which one guard was fatally shot. The Department of Corrections had banned Landon from visiting Lucas because of these allegations, even though they were proven false years ago. A Northern California judge recently lifted the ban after Landon filed suit with the Marin County Superior Court. Presently, Lucas is appealing his conviction.

Lucas appealed his conviction in 2014 and it was upheld by the State Supreme Court.

Danny Altstadt received psychiatric care while incarcerated and at least for many years did not remember murdering his parents and sister. His brother Gary, who was severely injured in the massacre, is managing all right in spite of his permanent impairments.

Update:

Inmate Hangs Himself 25 Years After Killing Most of Family

May 28, 2000 From Times Wire Services

A former Eagle Scout who killed his parents and sister and paralyzed his brother in a hatchet attack in their San Diego home 25 years ago was found hanged in his cell, authorities said.

Daniel Altstadt was pronounced dead at 4:07 a.m. Friday, Fresno County Deputy Coroner George Pimentel said Saturday.

That was about an hour after guards found him in a cell with a shoelace wrapped around his neck, said Lt. Rick Martinez of Pleasant Valley State Prison in Coalinga.

Efforts to revive him failed.

Altstadt, 43, arrived at the prison May 11 after being transferred from the lower-security California Men's Colony in San Luis Obispo, the *San Diego Union-Tribune* reported Saturday.

The transfer "was administrative, but there were disciplinary issues," Martinez told the newspaper.

Altstadt was assigned a private cell.

He had concerns for his well-being, for his own safety," said Martinez, who declined to elaborate.

He was not on suicide watch and had not shown any evidence of being a danger to himself, prison officials said.

Soon after sixteen-year-old Brenda Spencer was arrested for her early morning rampage, The Boom Town Rats put out a song describing her hatred of Mondays. Brenda has been making news lately by breaking her silence. She is trying trying to get a retrial for her sniper escapade that left two dead and many wounded. Brenda claims that she was intoxicated during the incident with alcohol and drugs, and can't remember what happened. She claims that during her trial she was heavily medicated by doctors. Doctors have testified that there was no PCP in her system during the shootings, as Brenda asserts, nor was there any alcohol. She expresses sorrow for the deaths and injuries, but the survivors, for the most part, don't want to ever see her get out. Brenda's father, Wally Spencer, married her cellmate.

An article in the *Daily Beast* dated May 30, 2014 stated that she feels partially responsible every time there is a school shooting. Maybe that remorse will lead to parole someday.

It would be plain stupidity to assume that these were isolated incidents that had no bearing on one another. Violence is a consuming fire that has no conscience, and with increased intensity, has no borders. It would be easy to dismiss what happened as merely the direct result of drug-induced insanity, but that is simply not the whole truth. It would be convenient to blame the violence on television and movies for these awful crimes. Although I firmly believe that both have a great role to play, it is not the whole answer. I do not believe that TV and media are a mere reflection of society. They are part of the storm that feeds on the sensational and the negative aspects of society. Drugs are instruments that assist in the searing of the conscience. But there is much more to it than this.

There has been a rapid destruction of the family unit over the past twenty-five years. In retrospect, it appears to be a carefully planned exercise. I am not easily persuaded by "conspiracy" philosophies, but I am convinced that there is something out there that is bent on destroying the positive aspects of a loving, nurturing environment. Gangs have replaced the family. In many instances these kids don't even know their fathers, so the acceptance and belonging they desire are fulfilled by joining up with their peers. The "higher" good is the 'hood or barrio, and killing to protect turf is expected. To many, the cops are just another gang infringing on their territory. There is no socio-economic group that is sheltered from gang activity.

Where the family falls short, the gang fills the vacuum.

It would be ignorance to deny the spiritual aspect of what is and has been happening. In spite of the bashing traditional family values have taken from the proponents of "alternate life-styles," the family unit was instituted by the same Creator who gave human society guidelines for living — written in stone. The family and society cannot continue without adhering to these absolutes.

Maybe humans really are like sheep. Sheep are probably the stupidest animals on the face of the earth. They would follow each other off of a cliff. They even need assistance to get back on their feet if they happen to fall over. There is a void in the human soul that craves direction and leadership. Unfortunately, society has become the leader, and we, like sheep, are blindly following its ever-changing value structure.

The human mind is like a computer ready to be programmed. When there are no absolutes, no guidelines, no boundaries, the mind will and can become programmed to its surroundings. When values fluctuate to fit the changing ebbs and flows of society, then society dictates conscience.

For example, Japan is still in a state of denial about World War II. Many Japanese feel that there are "no perpetrators, just victims." The Japanese history books have rewritten the truth to candy-coat the role their country played in the war. Their youth admittedly learn more about what really happened from sources outside their school environment.

Nazi Germany succeeded in duping what the world thought of as a cultured and intelligent society. Germans killed six-million Jews and "good" people just looked the other way.

Don't think that America is above this conscience-killing mind programming. What gives the Supreme Court the authority to say when life begins? America's future is erased from our hearts, minds, and memories in the name of convenience. We don't have the right to play God by saying, as some do, that this world is so bad that we shouldn't bring "unwanted" children into it. Rather, it is time to look at the family as a safe sanctuary that nurtures strength to face life head on.

Could there be a parallel between the Jews in Germany a half-century ago, and the voiceless unborn? These are just a couple of examples of the flimsiness of our foundation. When one group of people dictates what level of life is worth saving, and what isn't — we are in trouble.

When society as a whole diminishes the value of life, it is only reasonable to expect our children to follow suit. We have seen the innocence and aspirations of youth turn to a cold, merciless, pre-meditated culture of killing.

Distorted values, anti-heroes like the now-deceased Charlie Manson, and a discounting of the value of a human being have helped spread this type of violence.

Hopes for the future have been robbed by the lie that there is none. Could this been a covert act of the dark side, pushing its desire to crush the human soul? Or just a series of events that unfortunately fed on each other, causing disastrous results? Could a sensitive neighbor, counselor, parent, or friend have intervened in any of these lives and helped to prevent these tragic outcomes? Surely, just as negative influences from outside or within helped to distort reality to these young people, positive influences very well could have helped change the fate of every one of them.

Just as one person can ruin countless lives by an insane act, one person with a rational, loving heart can step out of his or her comfort zone to help, recognizing that all is not well with the world. It is impossible to predict when someone is going to flip out, but perhaps we can attempt to read between the lines and recognize trends that are not healthy. We cannot lay blame on parents, teachers, the media, peer pressure, and evil in general. We cannot depend on schools to establish values in our kids. We need to take back our families and our neighborhoods. We need to not look the other way. Then we can truly test the theory that good overcomes evil and love overcomes hate. This is not a simplistic solution; it is a goal for the long term.

You choose.

Soon after I first wrote this account of San Carlos and it's young people, my wife Maggie and I climbed to the top of Cowles Mountain. We found it hard to believe that where during our youth there had been no trail, just rough terrain where only the rugged would dare go before, joggers and babies on backpack now make the climb.

The view was very different from what was when my dad, my sister, and I made the climb. I can still see the ocean in the west, the Laguna Mountains in the east, and the golf course that used to be a grown-over valley. The landscape has grown up with the city, and large eucalyptus trees divide the neighborhoods.

It looked so peaceful down below. San Carlos had spread over many more miles with nice two-story homes crowded into areas where I used to ride my mini-bike and shoot birds with my BB gun. Santee, to the northeast, once the "boonies", now was crammed with houses, condos, and apartments. Lake Ariana, the street where my dad still lived, was hard to pick out because of the trees. Besides my wife, this seventy-two year old had become my best friend. We learned the key to forgiveness.

What seemed so strange was the fact that life goes on. Most of the people below in San Carlos never knew the insanity that once ruled their streets. The ones who did know carefully tucked it away in their memories. It's said that we never forget anything, but some things are stored more carefully than others. It must be a survival instinct

— I hope we can learn from our past.

Maggie and I said a short prayer that the Creator of the universe would look after this new generation of families. We closed with an "amen", and looked up to see the reflection of the sunset hitting a large white object on a hill in the southeast. The hill is Mt. Helix, and the white object was a cross that sits atop it. It is a peaceable overseer of the large valleys below.

We began our descent down the trail, which is direct but narrow. It is the best way down, because any other option is less certain. The potential for spraining an ankle, or worse, is high going down the wrong side. Perhaps, like those who climb mountains, we all need to learn by our mistakes. It is too late for some who chose the wrong path. The book of Romans describe them 2000 years ago: "Whose mouth is full of cursing and bitterness; their feet are swift to shed blood, destruction and misery are in their paths, and the path of peace have they not known. There is no fear of God in their eyes." (Romans 3:14-18, NAS Bible). In these times, the term "choice" is misused, but is applicable here. The psalmist writes of taking refuge in God by choosing the right road: "Thou will make known to me the path of life; In Thy presence is fullness of joy; In Thy right hand are pleasures forever." (Psalms 16:11, NAS Bible).

On this day, there wasn't a cloud in the sky — not even a suggestion of a puffy cirrus or cumulus anywhere.

Definitely, no hint of a dark, ominous thunderhead.

Maybe the thunderhead has travelled on. But what's to stop the storms of violence from visiting *your* neighborhood? What will you do when you see the dark specter silently creeping over your horizon? Will you pretend it doesn't exist, or that it will blow over? Or do you face the reality that you can play an active role in the lives around you? Don't fail to heed the warning signs!

CHAPTER 13

THE SURVIVORS

"I'm a survivor. I'm gonna make it." Destiny's Child

Twenty-four years have passed since the first edition of this book. During that time, beginning in 1997, I struggled with from Hepatitis C, no doubt as a result of my drug use. My liver got to such a low-functioning point that I only had the energy to get up and go to the bathroom. The words of my probation officer from years ago started to ring in my ear. "You are self-destructing," he said. I began to question in earnest the things I had done in my life. What caused me to do these things to myself? My liver deteriorated to stage-four fibrosis. Eventually, I was treated with Interferon and other cocktail drugs, which it addition to prayer, healed me.

I am one of the survivors.

Over the years, many things have brought hope and a sense of community to San Carlos. One of those is the creation of the San Carlos Survivors. It is a club for anyone who grew up or has lived in the community. It was created by Celeste Cecil Montalvo in 2002. She has put together events for the "survivors" on a yearly basis. She can be reached by email at scsurvivors@luckymail.com.

The vision statement is as follows:

"We are a neighborhood group of people who lived in the San Carlos, Del Cerro, and Allied Gardens communities during the 50's, 60's, 70's, 80's and beyond.

"Our purpose is to reunite old friends, make new friends, show respect and support for our communities, and celebrate our having been part of these San Diego areas.

"Our goal is to provide the opportunity for those who wish to reconnect with old friends, show our support to local businesses in our communities as well as supporting our Business Sponsors."

The Survivors have teamed up with Becky Green who has lived in the community for over sixteen years. She is working with the San Carlos Library spearheading a project called "San Carlos Gone By", gathering stories, photos, and memorabilia of San Carlos in days past. She is hosting regular events at the library. You can reach Becky at becky.green1202@gmail.com.

We hope the following success stories of San Carlos Survivors will be uplifting to you, or at least refresh some old memories:

Wendy Anderson — In the late '50s through the '60s, San Carlos was booming with new, affordable single-family housing. 99% of the buyers were families with children. It was the Mecca of the *Leave It To Beaver* kind of life.

Thousands of children packed all the schools. I went to Gage Elementary from 1964 to 1970. There were so many kids that the brand new school wasn't big enough. The district shipped in portable classrooms that were called bungalows to accommodate the students. Every class was packed.

Halloween was epic when we were kids. Kids were everywhere. Gage Elementary would have a carnival in its parking lot. There were games, homemade treats, and, unfortunately for the fish, goldfish in plastic bags as prizes. Our parents would let us go off with our friends to trick or treat. Every single house gave out candy, trinkets, fruit covered with something wonderful, and traditional candied apples.

Our parents didn't have to be afraid of poisons of any kind, pedophiles stealing their kids, or cars running us over. We were never given flashlights. If you were over eight or nine, and a parent wanted to tag along, it was embarrassing. As I got a little older, around eleven, pillow cases were the candy bag of choice. A lot of kids, particularly boys, would fill them until they were almost too heavy.

The Beatles, the Monkees, Procol Harum, the Doors and many others produced the music that was changing the world. The Viet Nam war was in full swing. Every household was touched by someone who got drafted. Older brothers and some dads were over there. The peace movement protesting the war was always in the news.

Another big news item was the Civil Rights Movement. My amazing parents supported it and taught me racism was wrong. Desegregation started when I was in junior high.

The '70s in San Carlos were infamous. Our parents were naive with no understanding of illegal drugs other than what was on the news. They trusted us. Thousands of us grew up in the era of "free love" and drugs were the thing. Our parents were clueless. They didn't have any warning or even the slightest chance to prepare for what was going to happen next. With inattentive parents, we were doing whatever we wanted. In any society, there is a percentage that gets into trouble. It seemed like there was a ridiculous amount of kids that went over the edge of civility.

The '70s were the times no one prepared for. I was thirteen in 7th grade at Pershing Jr. High. I was still fairly shy. I hated getting into trouble. I was a million times more naive than my folks. I was picked on by some all through my childhood. It escalated in 7th grade. I was terrified. They, (other girls), would surround me and throw stuff at me. I knew I had to come up with something. This was the beginning of a monster.

By the time I was in 8th grade, I had developed friendships that gave me an education my parents never could. I learned to be aggressive and ran around with a small gang. I'm not going to elaborate on what we did. I am ashamed of it.

One day was pivotal at Pershing. I was sitting in a class as my "Bad ass" self. It was hot and the door was opened. I saw boys picking on a more introverted boy. I left class, charged one offender making him stop, and comforted the kid who was the target. That experience brought me back to reality.

My high school boyfriend changed my world. He showed me how good life can be. He showed me things and goals I never dreamed of. It was then in the 10th grade my world changed forever.

I got straight A's for the first time. My parents were proud, if not a bit stupefied at the change.

I subsequently went to college and graduated. During that time I actually had the confidence being a "nerd". I felt like I was a rocket leaving the universe. The possibilities were endless.

There are literally thousands of people who came out of this crazy time and made something of themselves.

Forty and more years later, I am still friends with many San Carlosians and am extremely proud to be so. A lot of good came out of the mayhem. Even the most rough and tumble kids seemed to pull it together. San Carlos was an amazing place to grow up.

David Carroll — The name survivor means we got

through difficult times. I can say that while my memories of growing up there were not of the *Leave It To Beaver* kind, but more of struggles I got through. That's why I like this site. It shows that many San Carlosians we knew shared the same difficulties. It was life as we knew it for we knew no other. Some of us had it better off than others. Home life and guidance were different. Favorite memory: Poaching carp by the dam at Lake Murray and keeping it alive through the winter in our doughboy pool. Also, winning two fishing derbies at other local lakes when the season opened (with the same fish!).

Susie Stewart — Back in 1974 I lived on Ballinger Avenue and was the first *San Diego Union Tribune* papergirl. My dad got me the job after our paperboy threw our paper in our rose bushes nearly every day. My dad told the newspaper supervisor that "my daughter can throw a paper better and more accurate than the current deliverer." So, I got my first job. I got a second-hand Schwinn paper bike and went to work. Dad helped me on Sundays, and after we finished the route we would ride our bikes to Winchell's Donuts! Super great memories! My dad is now 79 years old. Oh yeah, how about polliwogs at the golf course!?

Toni Medawar Boyce — I grew up on Tommy Drive with my two sisters. My husband of 40 years is Steve Boyce. He grew up right across the street. We dated in junior high and high school and got married soon after. We both went to Gage Elementary, Pershing Jr. High, and Patrick Henry High. We had a great time "running amuck" and getting into trouble. Forty years, still in love and having a good time.

Mary Beth Asbury-Shipman — I lived on La Rouche Dr. at the top of Boulder Lake Drive. I remember playing all day and when it when it was getting to be dinner time, Mom called us home, not by cell phones but by yelling out our names and adding "Get home for dinner."

Jim Cox — In the early '70's when I was attending Pershing Jr. High, we lived across the street from Gage Elementary. One day I was walking our dog Taffy and a helicopter from Sea World went out to Gillespie Field to pick up some parts and on their return trip they passed over Gage. We were on Bisby Lake Dr. and the copter caught my attention. It was just over the power lines with the rotors pointing towards the ground. The copter came to rest in a side yard on Maury Ct. The pilots did not survive the crash. There were plenty of people who witnessed the crash and it was on the evening news. One of my memories was the rotor blade sticking out of the ground and most of the copter in a pile by the house.

Kathy Darnell — I didn't move to San Carlos until 1982. We lived on the corner of Blue Lake Drive and Lucerne for six months until the owners said they didn't want to sell. My parents then bought a home on Lake Badin. The owners of the Blue Lake home sold it six months later and my mom was not too happy about it. My parents still live on Lake Badin and love it. I remember climbing Cowles Mountain straight up not using a path. We walked everywhere — off campus at Patrick Henry High and up to the deli/hot dog place where Keil's Grocery now is. We also used to go to the Taco Bell on Wandermere.

Wendy Nickell Klusman — I remember walking around barefoot and our parents would let us play outside all day! You don't see that now. You could leave your house unlocked. I miss the good times back then.

Lori Linn Lyons — My friend Linda H. and I were hitch-hiking home from Patrick Henry and my mom pulled over and picked us up! OMG! The whole way home she whacked my legs saying "This feels a lot better than what some crazy person might have done to you!" Needless to say, I was put on restriction for the entire summer.

Dawn Gerber — I grew up on Balsam Lake Dr., went to Forward Elementary, Pershing Jr. High, and Patrick Henry

High. I remember playing hide and go seek after dark during summer. My brother played Little League Baseball and I worked the snack bar for free candy. We also took the bus to Mission Beach with our Boogie Boards during summer for twenty-five cents.

Frank C. Brtek Jr. — I remember catching polliwogs at the golf course. My house was above the 7th green. We caught them in the creek that ran from Cowles Mtn. Blvd. through the golf course. We also stole the golf carts and took them for joy rides!

Debbie Havens Grube — Great memories from the past, and bad memories getting arrested at seventeen for curfew. The best memories were ditching school and hanging out at the beach — and getting away with it!

Jeanne Hedman Fedak — We weren't allowed to swim in Lake Murray. It was against the law. It was closed for awhile due to a hydrilla infestation, so we swam all the time. We actually had rope swings hung in trees to jump off with into the water. There was still a ranger there, so you had to escape fast if you saw the truck coming. We would also build "igloo" forts out of the huge and plentiful tumbleweeds that blew around the area.

Kevin Shanty-Irish — How about driving cars and

trucks and motorcycles to the top of Cowles Mt. before they ended the fun by making it a park. That last curve before you got to the top was a doozy. I drove my 1973 Mazda RX-2 to the top along with a few motorcycles, including a 1968 Honda 90cc step-through-(no clutch).

Tamra Mendoza-Mode — Mary J. and I used to help the rec leaders check out balls in the rec center office. If they left us there alone we would chase each other around the desks in the rolling chairs.

Ramon Aguirre Montalvo — I grew up in Logan Heights but attended Lewis Jr. High and Henry, where I met my wife. We have raised our two boys here. San Carlos is very much a part of my youth, and where my future continues to unfold.

Michael Foley — I would like to remember the important work of Ann MacCullogh. She spearheaded the fight to stop the (SPSNOS) high rise, the formation of the San Carlos Area Council, the fight to stop the expansion of Jackson Drive, and much more. I have fond memories of those efforts. The character of the neighborhood stands strong today thanks to her work.

Margaret Sartain Hammon — One of my favorite memories is the long summers running and playing on

Cowles Mt. My family lived on Cowles Mt. Blvd. When I opened my back yard gate, all I could see was untouched nature and the mountain. There were rabbits and squirrels all over, and the not so likeable snakes and tarantulas. There was a natural stream that ran down the mountain and ended close behind our home. My siblings and neighbors would put our feet in the cool stream and catch polliwogs and tiny frogs all day. It was fun until someone would step on a cactus. This was before the apartments were built.

Michael Locke — I think it means something to all of us remembering our youthful time. Reminiscing with people we haven't seen in so many years, and also just remembering a great time in a great neighborhood with people we have never met, but were in the same place at the same time. We are all thankful that Celeste came up with this great idea and gave us this opportunity to re-experience this part of our lives.

Ted Stevenson — San Carlos means to me a safe, comfortable neighborhood where all eight of us siblings and our childhood friends ran amuck, laughed, learned everything we now know about family, friends, and life. I live away now but when I return to visit my parents who still live in the same house, it feels like I never left.

Celeste Teresa Cecil Montalvo-Jackson — I am proud to say that I am 3rd generation born and raised in San Diego from my father's side of the family. My father, Carlos G. Montalvo, graduated from San Diego High School. After serving in the USN during WWII, he married my Mamacita Esperanza (hope) Carvajal from Texas and they had three baby girls: Patricia Ann, Christine Marie, and Celeste Teresa.

They bought our San Carlos family home in 1959 when I was one-year-old. We are one of the few original owners still there. Even though I moved away in my twenties, I was blessed to have returned to my roots in 2000 with my husband Jack Jackson. We raised another generation with our sons Jared Riley and Clinton Travis. I am proud to announce that we now have a fourth generation baby girl being raised at "La Casa de Esperanza", named after my mother.

My father was a draftsman and I remember him telling me why he picked our house on Beaver Lake Drive, besides the lot and the layout of our casita. It was a newly developed middle class neighborhood and my parents felt it was a safe place to raise three daughters. I remember him saying he did not want us girls to ever feel discriminated and I certainly never did.

We were amongst the few Hispanics that lived in San Carlos at the time. You could bet our parents knew our friend's parents because there was usually more than one sibling in each family. Later in the years, my father worked for the Small Business Administration helping minorities obtain business loans so one way or another, whether it was the neighborhood, our schools, social organizations, sports, or the business community, our parents most likely knew one another.

Growing up in San Carlos, I attended John F. Forward Elementary, Pershing Junior High, and Patrick Henry High School, (both day and evening school). I also attended catechism at Our Lady of Grace church when I was a child.

I have great childhood memories. My favorite time was in elementary school. It started in kindergarten riding trikes around the circle, playing house, learning new games, and continued throughout the years with choir, skits, carnivals, after school movies, lunches, 6th grade camp, and graduation. We were the Forward Vikings and many of us are still life-long friends.

Our stomping grounds were about to change. The fields where we ventured out to explore and to catch polliwogs, ride bikes, etc., became baseball fields and the San Carlos Recreation Center. It was the home of Black Mountain Little League. The SCR offered lots of activities. I enjoyed the ceramics classes, playing ping pong, and hanging out at our new community playground.

I have great memories going out with my friends to movie theaters, drive-ins, and the Family Fun Center.

Around that time, they opened the House of Ice, where I would go ice skating on Friday nights. If you were lucky enough, parents would take you to the San Diego Zoo, Balboa Park, beaches, Belmont Park, or head east to Marshall Scotty's Playland Park, Big Oak Ranch for concerts, and Stallion Oak Ranch for camping.

So I went from my days at Forward playing games to my days in Jr. High playing hide-and-seek from the cops and helicopters. So if you heard the "Call of the Wild", the cops, then you would haul ass and hide. Little did I know back then the ice cream man sold more than popsicles and candy. The older boys were very accommodating and even shared their "ice cream" with us girls. We even ventured outside of the neighborhood to new stomping grounds at Mission Gorge Dam and Lake Murray Reservoir, but only to be chased away by the authorities, as we should have been.

By the time I was going into high school, our group was starting to change. Some moved away, others got locked up, and the unimaginable, some friends passed away. My parents got divorced so I became more rebellious, since my father was no longer in the house. I always seemed to gravitate towards the bad boys, so I traded my rock and roll and long haired hippie boys to disco and soul and low riders. Infinity Discoteque opened up in San Carlos, and it was a place we could go and listen to live bands, dance, and meet people outside of the neighborhood.

I graduated in the Class of 1977 from Patrick Henry Evening High School. Night school allowed me to work during the day. I remained in touch with my closest friends from elementary and junior high school, but lost touch with many classmates. I am so grateful that I moved back into my family home and reconnected with many childhood friends. As a result, San Carlos Survivors was formed. I have had the opportunity to meet many people from the neighborhood that I may not have otherwise. Our roots run deep and our friendships are for life.

Sincerely with love and peace to all, especially you survivors,

Celeste

A REQUEST

If you appreciate Mark's efforts to remember a distressing time and place in the quest to understand why it happened that way, please consider posting a brief review to your preferred online venue.

ALSO FROM HICKEY'S BOOKS

hickeybooks.com

by SUSAN SALGUERO:
The Gachi. She wasn't the only angry woman at U.C. Berkeley. Always on edge but unaware why, she knew she had to flee. A passion for music delivered her to Spain. There she staked her life on Flamenco.

by JARED BROWN:
Million Dollar Man. A phone call from a neighbor reporting a suspicious character at his home sends Jared Brown, a family man and Christian psychologist, to the outskirts of hell.

by ALAN RUSSELL & KEN KUHLKEN:
No Cats, No Chocolate. Mystery authors launch an adventure with high hopes and dreams of winning the fame they're convinced they deserve, as guests on a national television show. An Amazon #1 bestseller in several categories.

by OLGA SAVITSKY:
Shockabonda. Writers often imagine their ideal reader and compose accordingly. The reader Olga Savitsky chose was God. Since she wasn't likely to fool her reader, she needed to be real.

by KEN KUHLKEN:
Midheaven. High school senior Jodi McGee turns from drugs and

boys to Christ, but soon thereafter falls for her English teacher. As a result, tragedies test her will, her faith, and her sanity. Finalist for PEN's Ernest Hemingway Award for best first novel.

Reading Brother Lawrence. During a troubled time, novelist Ken Kuhlken discovered a certain book helped him find peace. *Reading Brother Lawrence* chronicles his search for understanding.

Write Smart. Much acclaimed author Ken Kuhlken shares insights gained over thirty-some years as a novelist, university creative writing professor, and founder of Perelandra College. By following the Write Smart process, writers will efficiently create, revise, and sell their stories.

Writing and the Spirit. Anastasia Campos declares "With all the ease of a friend on your couch-an ingenius, multiple-PhD-holding, wise-man sort of friend, Kuhlken combines observations of the world we live in, writers in history and his own experience (failures and triumphs) to form an all-around handbook of writerly wisdom."

by NICOLE L RIVERA:

Finding Unauthorized Faith in Harry Potter. Nicole L Rivera, Creative Team Manager for the fansite MuggleNet, marries faith with fandom in this wise and compelling devotional. Drawing on the Harry Potter story and parallels from the Bible, she reflects upon life's deepest truths, about faith, friendship, courage, loyalty, and love, and provides us with the keys to living like Christ and the Harry Potter heroes.

Hickey's Books provides support for the **Perelandra College writing programs** in the effort to enrich popular literature and writers' lives. Learn more at: perelandra.edu

ABOUT THE AUTHOR

Mark Stephen Clifton, a native San Diegan, is an award winning free-lance journalist. His articles have appeared in the *San Diego Reader*, *San Diego Union Tribune*, *San Diego Family Magazine*, and other local periodicals. He is the former president of Maranatha Surfing Association and holds a second-degree black belt in Tae Kwon Do from Ocean Beach Martial Arts Blue Wave School where he is a retired instructor.

He now lives in Bay Park with his wife, Maggie and is presently working on a novel that takes place in Ocean Beach.

Made in the USA
Las Vegas, NV
26 April 2024